CONRAD'S
HEART OF DARKNESS

CONTINUUM READER'S GUIDES

Achebe's Things Fall Apart – Ode Ogede

William Blake's Poetry – Jonathan Roberts

Dickens's Great Expectations – Ian Brinton

Fitzgerald's The Great Gatsby – Nicolas Tredell

Sylvia Plath's Poetry – Linda Wagner-Martin

CONRAD'S *HEART OF DARKNESS*

A Reader's Guide

ALLAN SIMMONS

CONTINUUM International Publishing Group
The Tower Building
11 York Road
London
SE1 7NX

80 Maiden Lane
Suite 704
New York,
NY 10038

First published 2007
Reprinted 2007

British Library Cataloguing-in-Publication Data
A catalogue record for this book is available from the British Library.

ISBN – 10: 0 8264 8933 8 (hardback)
0 8264 8934 6 (paperback)
ISBN – 13: 978 08264 8933 3 (hardback)
978 08264 8934 0 (paperback)

Library of Congress Cataloging-in-Publication Data
A catalog record for this book is available from the Library of Congress.

Typeset by Servis Filmsetting Ltd, Manchester
Printed and bound in Great Britain by
Biddles Ltd, King's Lynn, Norfolk

To Jethro

CONTENTS

QUOTATIONS AND ABBREVIATIONS

All references to Conrad's works are to *The Uniform Edition of the Works of Joseph Conrad*, 22 vols (London: J. M. Dent, 1923–8). References to Conrad's letters are to Laurence Davies *et al.* (eds), *The Collected Letters of Joseph Conrad*, 7 vols to date (Cambridge: Cambridge University Press, 1983–), or to G. Jean-Aubry, *Joseph Conrad: Life and Letters*, 2 vols, (London: Heinemann, 1927).

When quoting from letters, the following abbreviations are used:

CL = *The Collected Letters of Joseph Conrad*
LL = *Joseph Conrad: Life and Letters*

The following other abbreviation is used:

CCH = Sherry, Norman (ed.), *Conrad: The Critical Heritage*. (London: Routledge & Kegan Paul, 1973)

In quotations, a sequence of spaced points [. . .] indicates an ellipsis in the original text; a sequence of unspaced points [...] an elision that I have made.

CHAPTER 1

CONTEXTS

BIOGRAPHY

1. Polish Context: The Ukraine, Russia and Austrian Poland

Joseph Conrad was the adopted name of Józef Teodor Konrad Korzeniowski. He was born on 3 December 1857 at Berdichev, in Podolia, a part of the Polish Commonwealth that had become part of the Russian Ukraine in 1793. The Polish Republic would only be reinstated in 1918, after the First World War. Conrad's homeland was thus not a geographical fact but a country of the heart. When he was four years old, his parents, Apollo and Ewelina (Ewa), were arrested for clandestine political activities against Tsarist rule and incarcerated in the infamous Warsaw Citadel, whose later occupants included 'Red' Rosa Luxemburg, imprisoned during the 1905 Russian Revolution. Conrad later recalled: 'in the courtyard of this Citadel – characteristically for our nation – my childhood memories begin' (*CL*1: 358). An only child, in May 1862 he accompanied his parents into imposed exile to Perm in the Urals, and then to Vologda, some 300 miles east of St Petersburg. Unsurprisingly in these harsh climatic conditions, Conrad was sickly, and would be dogged by illness for the rest of his life.

In January 1863, the Korzeniowskis were again moved, to Chernikhov, north east of Kiev, as news of the failed insurrection in Poland filtered out. Ewa's health became a matter of concern and she was granted a three-month reprieve for medical attention and to visit relatives. Conrad's first known composition dates from this time. Written on the back of a photograph sent to his maternal grandmother, it reads: 'To my beloved Grandma who helped me send cakes to my poor Daddy in prison', and is signed 'grandson, Pole-Catholic, nobleman, Konrad' (Najder ed., 1964: 8). It is dated 6 July 1863, when Conrad was just five and a half years old.

Ewa Korzeniowska's health steadily deteriorated and she died in April 1865, leaving Conrad to the care of his father, whom he remembered as a 'man of great sensibilities; of exalted and dreamy temperament; with a terrible gift of irony and of gloomy disposition; withal of strong religious feeling degenerating after the loss of his wife into mysticism and despair' (*CL*2: 247). Understandably, these experiences left Conrad with a lifelong antipathy to things Russian. They did, however, provide him with an early contact with literature, as his father translated works by Shakespeare, Dickens and Victor Hugo, and read aloud Polish romantic poetry. Conrad's own ill-health necessitated various treatments, in Kiev and Żytomierz, as Kozeniowski, sustained by an allowance from his brother-in-law, Tadeusz Bobrowski, struggled to oversee the education of the 'little orphan' (Najder ed., 1983: 102).

In late 1867, and himself now ailing, Apollo Korzeniowski was granted permission to leave Chernikov. Initially settling in Lemberg in Austrian Poland (now Lviv in Ukraine) in February 1868, a year of wandering, that included medical treatment, ensued. But Korzeniowski was nearing his end, writing in October 1868: 'I am broken, fit for nothing, too tired even to spit upon things' (Najder ed., 1983: 120). He died in May 1869 in Cracow, his funeral procession becoming a patriotic demonstration as it wound through the streets of the old city with the eleven-year-old Conrad at its head. Apollo Korzeniowski's gravestone bears the inscription: 'the victim of Muscovite tyranny.'

Care of 'Konradek' settled on his maternal uncle, Tadeusz Bobrowski, who oversaw his nephew's education and financial affairs, and continued to provide support and advice until his death in 1894. Conrad described his standing with his uncle as 'more in the relation of a son than a nephew' (*CL*2: 246), and his first novel, *Almayer's Folly* (1895), is dedicated 'To the memory of T. B.' Although little is known of Conrad's early education, his reading included sea and travel writers, such as Frederick Marryat, James Fenimore Cooper and Mungo Park, alongside such novels as Dickens's *Bleak House* (1852–3), Cervantes's *Don Quixote* (1605, 1615), Hugo's *Les Travailleurs de la mer* (1866), and Turgenev's *Smoke* (1867). Of his schooling he would later admit 'a latent devotion to geography which interfered with my devotion (such as it was) to my other schoolwork' (*Last Essays*: 12). In the same essay, 'Geography and Some Explorers', Conrad identifies himself as 'a contemporary of the Great Lakes' (14) and records an incident that earned him the derision of his school friends: 'One day, putting my finger on a spot in the very middle of the then white heart of Africa, I declared that some day I would go there' (16). This boast would be realized eighteen years later when Conrad stood on the deck of 'a wretched little stern-wheel steamboat' near the Stanley Falls on the Congo River.

2. The Sea

In 1874 Bobrowski acceded to his nephew's request to go to sea and secured him a position with a shipping firm, C. Delestang et Fils, in Marseilles. The Korzeniowskis were minor gentry, belonging to the Polish *szlachta* class, so French was Conrad's second language. As he later told John Galsworthy, it was in Marseilles that 'the puppy opened his eyes' (*CL*3: 240). Conrad made three voyages to the Caribbean in Delestang's ships, learning the craft that he would serve for nearly twenty years. It was in Marseilles harbour that Conrad heard himself addressed in English for the first time, 'the speech of my secret choice, of my future, of long friendships, of the deepest affections, of hours of toil and hours of ease, and of solitary hours too, of books read, of thoughts pursued, of remembered emotions – of my very dreams!' (*A Personal Record*: 136). In April 1878 Conrad joined a British ship, the *Mavis*, bound for the Sea of Azov via Constantinople, as an unofficial apprentice, beginning his career in the British Merchant Service.

Disembarking from the *Mavis* in Lowestoft on 10 June 1878, Conrad touched English soil for the first time. Nicknamed

'Polish Joe', he served as an ordinary seaman in the *Skimmer of the Sea*, making voyages between Lowestoft and Newcastle. Conrad later recalled this experience as a 'Good school for a seaman', adding: 'In that craft I began to learn English from East Coast chaps each built as though to last for ever, and coloured like a Christmas card' (*CL*2: 35). Then, in October 1878, he signed on in the wool-clipper *Duke of Sutherland*, bound for Australia, beginning his international shipping career in British ships.

Conrad's career in the merchant fleet lasted fifteen years, in the heyday of the British Empire which, at its peak, extended to a quarter of the globe and when Britannia ruled the waves. The British Merchant Service was the workhorse of Empire, and the nation's inability to meet the demand for sailors meant that foreigners were not uncommon in the ranks. In one sense, Britain was imperialist because she had to be economically. Her maritime dominance ensured that she was the world's trader, and her economic supremacy was directly linked to overseas markets and sources of primary products. By the time of the Boer War of 1899–1902, Britain was dependent upon imports for two-thirds of her food, and British shipping accounted for half of the world's tonnage. According to Eric Hobsbawm, access to the non-European world was, simply, 'a matter of life and death for the British economy' (2002: 74). By his own definition 'a Polish nobleman, cased in British tar' (*CL*1: 52), he steadily worked his way up through the ranks, acquiring his captain's certificate in 1886, the same year in which he became a naturalized Briton, subject of Queen Victoria rather than Tsar Alexander III. Writing to Jozef Spiridion, also of Polish descent, in October 1885, Conrad claimed: 'When speaking, writing or thinking in English the word Home always means for me the hospitable shores of Great Britain' (*CL*1: 12).

Conrad saw the world in the last great age of sailing ships as they inevitably gave way to steam, reflecting the truism that technology was the great fact in the story of Empire. His sea experiences provided the source for much of his fiction, leading Henry James to comment in 1906: 'No one has *known* – for intellectual use – the things you know, and you have, as the artist of the whole matter, an authority that no one has approached' (Edel ed., 1984: 419). In particular, Conrad's writings ensure that he will forever be associated with the seas and islands of the Malay Archipelago. While serving in a trading steamer, the *Vidar*, in 1887, Conrad visited the Malay settlement of Berau in east Borneo, where he met the Eurasian trader Willem Carel Olmeijer, prototype for the central character of his first novel. Conrad later recorded: 'if I had not got to know Almayer pretty well it is almost certain there would never have been a line of mine in print' (*A Personal Record*: 87). In 1890, Conrad went to the Congo Free State, having been promised the command of a steamboat on the Congo River. In the event, the command never materialized, but his experiences provided the material for *Heart of Darkness*.

The expertise Conrad gained as a professional seaman in the merchant fleet served his writing in other forms, too. For instance, *The Mirror of the Sea*, published in 1906, consists of a number of essays on aspects of sea life; while his occasional writings – collected in *Notes on Life and Letters* (1921) and *Last Essays* (published posthumously in 1926) – include essays on the *Titanic* disaster of 1912, and on the role played by the Merchant Service during the First World War. In his 'Author's Note' to *The Mirror of the Sea* Conrad identified 'the ultimate shapers of my character, convictions, and, in a sense, destiny' as 'the imperishable sea, ... the ships that are no more, and ... the simple men who have had their day' (xii). It was during a voyage to Australia in 1892–3 in the *Torrens*, one of the fastest ships of her day, that Conrad's manuscript of *Almayer's Folly* had its first reader, W. H. Jacques, a Cambridge man travelling to Australia for his health, whose pronouncements on the tale left Conrad feeling 'as if already the story-teller were being born into the body of a seaman' (*A Personal Record*: 17). Conrad's sea career ended in 1894 when he signed off the *Adowa*.

3. The Writing-Desk

Beginning with *Almayer's Folly* in 1895, Conrad's career as a professional writer lasted nearly thirty years, until his death in 1924. During this time, and writing in his third language, after Polish and French, he published roughly one volume per year. Shortly after the publication of his second novel, *An Outcast of the Islands*, a prequel to *Almayer's Folly* and published the following year, Conrad married Jessie George. After a prolonged honeymoon in Brittany, they settled in Stanford-le-Hope in Essex, close to Conrad's first English friend and fellow seafarer, G. F. W. Hope, whose yawl, the *Nellie*, Conrad immortalized as the setting for Marlow's tale in *Heart of Darkness*. The Conrads, who had two sons, Borys and John, moved house frequently, occupying eight rented homes, all in southern England, mainly in Kent – 'in the depths of the country, out of ear-shot of gossips, beyond reach of hostesses', as Virginia Woolf observed (1942: 282).

Conrad's writing quickly earned the acclaim of fellow professionals, including Henry James, H. G. Wells and Ford Madox Ford, and he collaborated with the latter on three novels, *The Inheritors*, *Romance* and *The Nature of a Crime*. Popular success, however, eluded him. The masculine tenor of his fiction, with its maritime, colonial, and political settings, may have accounted for some of this neglect. As early as 1896 Wells chided: 'you don't make the slightest concessions to the reading young woman who makes or mars the fortunes of authors' (Stape and Knowles, eds, 1996: 21). Significantly, when financial success came, it was for *Chance* (1914), whose subject, the entrapment of woman in patriarchal society, capitalized on public interest in the 'woman question'.

After two novels set against the backdrop of the Dutch East Indies, Conrad next turned his attention to the maritime world, and in *The Nigger of the 'Narcissus'* (1897) and '*Typhoon*' (1902) established himself as our greatest writer of the sea. This rich vein also yielded the Marlow trilogy of 'Youth' (1898), *Heart of Darkness* (1899) and *Lord Jim* (1900) in which an increasingly confident Conrad brings the English seaman-narrator's views to bear upon the colonial world. There followed the three great political novels, *Nostromo* (1904), *The Secret Agent* (1907) and *Under Western Eyes* (1911), set respectively in South America, London, and St Petersburg and Geneva. Audacious in their scope and meditation, these are often considered to be the apex of Conrad's achievement.

Never able to live within his means, the first two decades of Conrad's writing life were punctuated by protestations of impoverishment, dependence upon the generosity of friends, like John Galsworthy, and literary institutions – he received awards from the Royal Literary Fund (in 1902, 1904 and 1908), the Royal Bounty Fund (in 1905), and, in 1910, was granted a Civil List pension of £100 annually – and mounting debts, especially to his long-suffering agent, J. B. Pinker; to the extent where Conrad realized that 'those books which, people say, are an asset of English literature owe their existence to Mr Pinker as much as to me' (*CL5*: 619). Of financial necessity, Conrad became adept at exploiting the burgeoning literary marketplace. During his honeymoon, he turned his hand to writing shorter fiction as a lucrative means of supplementing his income from novels. This form yielded a much greater return for effort: for instance, in 1901, when average earnings were around £100 per annum, Conrad earned £40 for 'Amy Foster', a story of 12,500 words. Spanning 20 years of his career as a writer, Conrad's novellas and short stories run to seven volumes. The boom in literary magazines also meant that an author could expect multiple payments for the same piece of work from the sale of serial and book rights, both in Britain and abroad.

Following *Chance*, *Victory* (1915) and *The Shadow-Line* (1917) also recorded outstanding sales, despite being published during the First World War, in which the Conrads' eldest son, Borys, saw service and suffered shell shock. Although they sold well, the late novels – *The Arrow of Gold* (1919), *The Rescue* (1920) and *The Rover* (1923) – reveal a creatively exhausted author writing increasingly melodramatic fiction. With no little irony, popular and financial recognition came after most of the work for which Conrad remains famous had been written. But when it came, the turnaround in Conrad's fortunes was phenomenal.

In the closing years of his life, and now the elder statesman of English letters, Conrad's reputation ensured that his manuscripts and typescripts attracted collectors, and, in 1919, the sale of the film rights to four of his novels netted a cool $20,000. He signed contracts for collected editions of his works in England and the United States; stage versions of his novels were performed (with little success); several of his works had appeared in French translation; and, in 1923, he undertook a promotional tour of America where he was publicly lionized. He died of a heart attack on 3 August 1924, and was buried four days later in Canterbury Cemetery.

CONTEXTS

1. Historical

When Conrad was born, in 1857, Queen Victoria was celebrating her twentieth year on the throne. Her reign would continue for over forty years, lasting until her death in January 1901, by which time the British Empire subsumed a quarter of the world's population. Monarch and emblem, Victoria gave her name to the era in which Britain was transformed from being the workshop of the world into its banker. In the year of Conrad's death, 1924, Europe was still recovering from the First World War (1914–18), the Bolshevik Revolution had succeeded in Russia (1917) and the Irish Free State had come into being (1921). This was also the year in which Ramsay MacDonald was elected prime minister of Britain's first Labour government.

Serendipity and historical coincidence combined to link Joseph Conrad to the British Empire, and at a moment when colonialism was replaced by the more systematic imperialism. He shares the year of his birth, 1857, with Sir Edward Elgar, whose music captured and contributed towards the popular patriotic mood of the country. But 1857 was also the year of the Indian Mutiny. Sometimes regarded as the first step towards a united independence movement in India, the rising is remembered as much for the challenge posed to imperial rule – slight, as it turned out – as for the ruthlessness of British reprisals. As a result of the mutiny, responsibility for administering the subcontinent passed from the East India Company to the Crown. Queen Victoria was proclaimed 'Empress of India' on New Year's Day 1877.

Empire was the dominant fact of British life in the late nineteenth century, as Rudyard Kipling, the great poet of imperialism, enjoined his countrymen to 'Take up the White Man's Burden'. It dominated the British political scene, characterized in the second half of the nineteenth century by alternating Liberal ('Whig') and Conservative governments, under William Gladstone and Benjamin Disraeli, respectively, until Gladstone's decision to espouse the cause of Home Rule for Ireland split the Liberal Party in 1886, resulting in twenty years of virtually uninterrupted Conservative rule, sustained by an anti-Gladstone, anti-Home Rule alliance. With Empire the currency of political debate, Gladstonian Liberalism was perceived as anti-imperial. By contrast, the Conservatives were the party of Empire. Disraeli enhanced this view through, among other things, the purchase of shares in the Suez Canal, gaining a controlling interest for Britain in 1875. And Gladstone himself, in his 1878 essay 'England's Mission', had declared: 'The sentiment of empire may be called innate in every Briton. If there are exceptions, they are like those of men born blind or lame among us.' But while the international, colonial world of 'Greater Britain' helped to formulate a sense of the identity of Great Britain, by the turn of the century dissenting voices were also beginning to be heard, and where Kipling asked rhetorically 'What can they know of England who only England know?', G. K. Chesterton responded with a rhetorical question of his own: 'What can they know of England who only know the world?' (1928: 42).

By the nineteenth century's close, Britain's role as the global economic superpower was under threat from the United States, resurgent after the Civil War of 1861–5, and, closer to home, from an increasingly expansionist Germany. An alternative view of empire was gradually emerging, one that foresaw its passing and posed a challenge to it. The history of British imperial expansion across the century includes a number of setbacks that led to criticism of empire at home. If military progress in the Crimean War, fought against Poland's enemy, Russia, midway through the century, raised questions about the competence of the ruling elite, then events such as the Indian Mutiny in 1857, or the death of General Gordon in Khartoum in 1885, inevitably entrenched the views of both pro- and anti-imperialists. The Boer War of 1899–1902, which Kipling viewed as 'the first battle in the war of 14–18' (Lycett, 1999: 296–7), provides a good example.

Used to fighting colonial wars against poorly armed natives, the British found the Boers well armed by Germany. None the less, Britain's superior armaments ensured that, by 1900, the main Boer cities had been captured. Victory seemed certain – so much so that Salisbury easily won the so-called 'Khaki election' that year – but the Boers refused to surrender and resorted to guerrilla tactics. The British response was to burn Boer farmsteads and herd the women and children into 'concentration camps'. It backfired when the high death toll in the camps led to public protests at home, ensuring that victory, when it came, was a pyrrhic one.

The fact of empire was demonstrably incommensurate with the means used to sustain it. To the pro-imperialists, the Boer War demonstrated the strength of empire: her white settler colonies sent troops to help – some 30,000 came from Canada, New Zealand and Australia; to the anti-imperialists it demonstrated that the British Empire was over-extended and under-coordinated. Added to this, a high proportion of working-class volunteers were discovered to be simply too under-nourished to be acceptable cannon fodder. *The Oxford History of Britain* summarized the repercussions of the Boer War: 'military ineffectiveness and the poor quality of recruits in the South African war led to a public cry among the propertied classes for a reappraisal of the economic, social, and even political arrangements of the nation as a whole' (Matthew and Morgan, 1992: 49).

Of specific relevance to *Heart of Darkness* is the 'Scramble for Africa' in the late nineteenth century. Before then, as place names like Ivory Coast, Gold Coast and Slave Coast crudely witness, European involvement in the continent was largely exploitative. But across the century the interior of the so-called 'Dark Continent' was steadily mapped by explorers and missionaries. In 1871, and two years before his death, while searching for the source of the Nile, Livingstone stumbled upon the Lualaba River; five years later, while attempting to cross Africa from east to west, Stanley showed this to be the source of the River Congo. On this expedition he became the first white man to sail down the Congo. Such pioneering exploration was quickly overtaken by imperialist exploitation, as European powers were attracted to

Africa's resources. By the mid-1870s, beyond coastal trading posts and a few strategically important colonies, such as South Africa, which safeguarded Britain's access to the Indian Ocean and the lucrative spice trade, most of the continent remained mysterious. With incredible speed, by 1900 virtually all of Africa had been appropriated and pillaged by European powers. For instance, in just 18 months, between 1883 and 1885, South West Africa, Togoland, the Cameroons and East Africa all came under German rule, their colonization characterized by Foreign Minister Bernard von Bülow, in 1897, as his country's right to 'a place in the sun'.

In 1876, King Leopold II of Belgium founded the International African Association, with himself as its president. Ostensibly a crusade against the slave trade within the continent, Leopold emphasized the nobility of the venture: 'To open to civilization the only part of our globe where it has yet to penetrate, to pierce the darkness which envelops whole populations, it is, I dare to say, a crusade worthy of this century of progress.' Behind this, however, lay his real intentions, expressed in a letter to his London Ambassador shortly afterwards: 'I do not want to miss a good chance of getting us a slice of this magnificent African cake' (Pakenham, 1991: 21, 22). Given that *Heart of Darkness* played its part in exposing the atrocities perpetrated in the Congo Free State, it is no small historical irony that the steamboat in which Conrad served was named the *Roi des Belges* (King of the Belgians). Belgium itself had no colonial aspirations, but Leopold persuaded the European powers, themselves wary of rival competitors in Africa, to accept him, apparently a philanthropic neutral, as owner and ruler of the 'Congo Free State' in 1885. The country, an area almost eighty times as large as Belgium, became Leopold's personal fiefdom, and he appointed Henry Stanley as his chief agent, responsible for establishing steamer routes, signing treaties with native chiefs and setting up a chain of commercial and scientific stations that, once garrisoned, were nothing less than armed outposts of Empire.

As *Heart of Darkness* reveals, the Congo Free State was rich in ivory. Of even greater value to industrial Europe at the dawn of the motor car age were its equatorial forests of rubber trees. It was for this commodity above all that untold Congolese lives – some estimate ten million – were sacrificed to the king's greed in an orgy of brutality and exploitation. Conrad described what he saw in the Congo in 1890 as 'the vilest scramble for loot that ever disfigured the history of human conscience' (*Last Essays*: 17). While there, he met Roger Casement, who became British Consul for the Congo Free State in 1898. Equally appalled, Casement campaigned tirelessly against Leopold's reign, investigating its atrocities and broadcasting his findings in a report of 1904. (Knighted for his humanitarian efforts, Casement would expose similar atrocities – also in the pursuit of rubber – against the Putumayo Indians in the Amazon jungles six years later.) With Leopold brought to the bar of international opinion for his crimes, the Belgian government voted to relieve their king of his African territory, annexing the Congo Free State in 1908.

What Conrad must have made of the historical irony by which he, a refugee from Russian imperialism, came to serve in the merchant navy of the world's greatest empire, can only be guessed. Marlow's view of European expansion in *Heart of Darkness*, however, is damning: 'The conquest of the earth, which mostly means the taking it away from those who have a different complexion or slightly flatter noses than ourselves, is not a pretty thing when you look into it too much' (50–1). Conrad's career in the British Merchant Marine made him an ideal intermediary between the Western and exotic worlds. In this he was not alone: the French writer Pierre Loti was another professional mariner turned author, and, in English letters, colonial administrators like Rider Haggard and colonial journalists like Rudyard Kipling also drew upon personal experiences for their fiction.

2. Intellectual

Intellectually, Conrad's is the age that absorbs and responds to the influences of Charles Darwin (1809–82), Karl Marx (1818–83) and Sigmund Freud (1856–1939), and whose prevailing mood of scepticism is starkly voiced in Nietzsche's claim, made in *Thus Spake Zarathustra* (1883–91), that 'God is dead'. In the face of such opposition to inherited beliefs – religious, social and individual – it is unsurprising that Gabriel Conroy in

James Joyce's 'The Dead' (in *Dubliners*, 1914) should describe himself as living 'in a sceptical' and 'thought-tormented age' (232). Darwin's *The Origin of Species* (1859) undermined a key argument for the existence of God by demonstrating that the blind processes of random variation and natural selection could combine to counterfeit design in the natural world. An English naturalist, Darwin applied his theory of evolution by natural selection to man in *The Descent of Man* (1871), with the unfortunate consequence that, in its adapted form, known as 'social Darwinism', biology was linked to ideology to provide a pseudoscientific defence of racial superiority.

In *The Communist Manifesto* (1848), written with Friedrich Engels, Marx asserted the fundamental importance of the class struggle, arguing that, in the face of inhumane working conditions, the proletariat would revolt and overthrow the landowning bourgeoisie. Its famous opening sentence, 'The history of all hitherto existing society is the history of class struggles', provided the rallying call for social revolutions in the second half of the nineteenth century, and the annual May Day demonstrations held to assert working-class internationalism were inaugurated in 1890. German by birth, Marx moved to England in 1849 and developed his theories of the class struggle and the economics of capitalism to argue that human actions and institutions are economically determined, that the class struggle is the basic agency of historical change, and that capitalism will ultimately be superseded by communism. These form the basis of *Das Kapital* (1867, 1885, 1895), written in the British Museum Reading Room, and are embellished by examples of the conditions that Marx witnessed among the English working classes.

If, at their most extreme, Darwin and Marx reduce the individual to a puppet of biology or history, irresistibly caught up in the power struggle of natural selection or class conflict, then Freud extended these revolutionary challenges to inherited belief to the unconscious itself. The originator of psychoanalysis, which is based upon the free association of ideas and the analysis of dreams, Freud argued that dreams, like neuroses, offer disguised manifestations of repressed desires, generally of a sexual origin. Stressing the importance of infantile sexuality in later development, he formulated the theory of the Oedipus Complex, by means of which identity itself is rendered precarious within a concealed narrative of sexual development, and later proposed that the mind can be conceptualized as a tripartite psychic apparatus, composed of the id, the ego, and the superego, a model that challenged the established Cartesian identification of the mind with consciousness. Freud's writings, including *The Interpretation of Dreams* (1900), published a year after *Heart of Darkness*, and *The Ego and the Id* (1923), ensured that such ideas as the unconscious, libido, repression, the Oedipus Complex, and even the adjective Freudian quickly became popular currency. Freud's legacy is conveyed by W. H. Auden in a poem written shortly after his death: 'To us he is no more a person / Now but a whole climate of opinion' ('In Memory of Sigmund Freud').

Contemporary artists, with their sensitive antennae, recognized theirs as a transfigured era, commenting, often with self-conscious prescience, upon the passing of an old world. According to Virginia Woolf, 'in or about December 1910 human character changed' (1981: 91), while D. H. Lawrence, who warned the critic Edward Garnett, 'You mustn't look in my novel for the old stable *ego* of the character. There is another *ego*, according to whose action the individual is unrecognisable' (letter of 5 June 1914), claimed apocalyptically: 'It was in 1915 the old world ended. In the winter 1915–1916 the spirit of the old London collapsed; the city, in some way, perished, perished from being the heart of the world, and became a vortex of broken passions, lusts, hopes, fears, and horrors' (*Kangaroo*: 220). Capturing this prevailing sense of crisis, Conrad depicted human nature as, fundamentally, alienated within a purposeless universe, in an early letter to Cunninghame Graham: 'Life knows us not and we do not know life – we don't even know our own thoughts. Half the words we use have no meaning whatever and of the other half each man understands each word after the fashion of his own folly and conceit. Faith is a myth and beliefs shift like mists on the shore; thoughts vanish; words, once pronounced, die; and the memory of yesterday is as shadowy as the hope of to-morrow' (*CL*2: 17).

3. Cultural

As Christian certainty faltered in the wake of the Darwinian revolution, so science provided a modern mythology, supplying the ideas that shape human knowledge. For instance, Albert Einstein (1879–1955), the greatest theoretical physicist of his age, proposed the special theory of relativity in 1905 and the general theory of relativity in 1916. Impossibly recondite to the layman, these theories, according to which time is relative, space is curved, and light does not travel in straight lines, revised human understanding of the universe, making Einstein world famous and his name a byword for superior intelligence. Less abstract evidence of the scale and rate of technological change in this age is ubiquitous. For example, Conrad's first novel, *Almayer's Folly*, shares its year of publication, 1895, with the invention of the telephone and the discovery of X-rays by Röntgen. The novel itself, though set in Borneo, also features the gramophone, a sign of the future global village that would emerge after Conrad's lifetime. This was also the year in which Freud published his first work on psychoanalysis and Marconi sent his first message over a mile by wireless.

Advances in Western technology also bore heavily upon global politics. Steamships and telegraph cables connected distant parts of the world, while the first automatic machine gun, invented by Hiram Maxim in 1884, led to ludicrously one-sided battles with colonial enemies: in the decisive defeat of the Mahdists in 1898, 10,000 Sudanese were killed at the Battle of Omdurman at a cost to General Kitchener of just 48 men. As Hilaire Belloc put it in 'The Modern Traveller' (1898): 'Whatever happens, we have got / The Maxim Gun, and they have not.' Closer to home, the technological advances of the age were tempered by despair, too. In April 1912, the 'unsinkable' White Star liner *Titanic* struck an iceberg and sank on her maiden voyage, while the battlefields of the First World War saw death and destruction on an industrial scale, previously unimaginable.

By the turn of the century, social transformation was everywhere apparent: when Victoria ascended the throne, the population was predominantly rural; by the time of her death, three-quarters of it was urban. The old rural way of life gave way to an industrial working class increasingly taking on a political shape. In 1900, the Trades Union Congress supported the founding of a Labour Representative Committee, forerunner of the Labour Party. And while the dock strike of 1889, the rail strike of 1911 and the coal strike the following year seemed to raise the spectre of 'mob rule' a century after the French Revolution, the increasing militancy of the suffragettes interrogated the assumptions of patriarchal society. In 1902, Arthur Griffiths formed Sinn Fein ('ourselves alone') to promote the cause of Irish independence. Included in these social revolutions was the establishment of an increasingly literate population thanks to successive Education Acts between 1870 and 1893. More subtly, the era of popular mass culture had begun: mass circulation newspapers, tea-drinking, fish and chips, football and cricket, music hall and, later, the cinema – all have their origins in this period. The first public showing of film, by the brothers Lumière, was in 1895.

The formative strains of the twentieth century were being heard in the arts, too. Musically, for instance, these were the years of Elgar, Delius and Vaughan Williams at home, while, on the Continent, Offenbach's *La Vie Parisienne* dominated the spirit of 'Gay Paree' and Johann Strauss II ensured that Vienna remained the home of the waltz. But other, more atonal notes were being sounded, disrupting the aural perspective of traditional harmony. For example, in Debussy's impressionistic *La Mer* (1905), musical 'plot' is replaced by an emphasis upon mood. These were the years of Arnold Schoenberg's *Pierrot Lunaire* (1912), the early works of Alban Berg and Anton Webern, and the cause célèbre of Igor Stravinsky's *The Rite of Spring* (1913) that gave an avant-garde inflection to this pagan rite and, choreographed by Vaslav Nijinsky, caused a riot when it premièred in Paris. Conrad may share his birth year with Elgar, but in the year of his death, 1924, George Gershwin's combination of classical music and jazz, *Rhapsody in Blue*, was first performed.

While music challenged traditional, inherited expectations of tonality and harmony, the visual arts were no less innovative, subverting perspective itself. Cubism altered mimetic representation, rearranging pictorial planes to formulate a new relationship between form and content, between the perceiver and the object perceived. Modernist painting is characterized by the splintering of nineteenth-century realist traditions into a range of, often radical, 'isms', each with its own 'manifesto'. Thus the period, which charted the transformation from Impressionism to Cubism, includes Fauvism, Pointillism, Symbolism, Expressionism, Dadaism, Surrealism and Futurism, and its enduring legacy derives from such figures as Cézanne, Van Gogh, Matisse, Seurat, Munch, Klimt, Braque and Picasso, whose *Les demoiselles d'Avignon* was first exhibited in 1907, the year of the first Cubist exhibition, in Paris. The iconoclasm of the age is evident in Marcel Duchamp's submission of a urinal, *Fountain*, to an exhibition of Independent Artists in 1917. With hindsight, these aesthetic revolutions take on political significance: with their emphasis upon subjective interpretation, forms such as Impressionism, Symbolism and Cubism pose a challenge to early-twentieth-century forces of collectivism, measured in jingoist nationalism or revolutionary communism.

Enjoined by Ezra Pound to 'Make It New', the authors of the period shared in this revolution. Modernist literature is characterized by formal and technical experimentation. Reflecting some of the innovations made in the other arts, its emphasis falls on impressionism and subjectivity – on *how* rather than *what* we see, perhaps most exemplified by the art theorist and painter Roger Fry, who in a lecture on a picture featuring the crucifixion referred to the subject only as 'the central colour mass'; the apparent objectivity of the nineteenth-century omniscient narrator is increasingly eschewed in favour of a fluctuating or individual point of view, with a resultant weakening of clear-cut moral positions; and fragmentation becomes a virtue rather than a vice, yielding 'cubist' narratives dependent for their coherence upon juxtaposition rather than the causal demands of plot, a technique T. S. Eliot exploited in his long poem *The Waste Land* (1922). In a letter of 1922, Virginia Woolf declared that 'our generation must . . . renounce finally . . . the beauty that comes from completeness' (1993: 154).

4. Literary

Conrad's first audience was weaned on Dickens: *Little Dorrit* was published in the year of his birth – so was Flaubert's *Madame Bovary*. He died two years after the publication of James Joyce's *Ulysses* and T. S. Eliot's *The Waste Land*, the twin peaks of high Modernism in English literature that his own writings had helped to fashion. In a letter to William Blackwood, who first published *Heart of Darkness*, Conrad declared: 'I am *modern*', comparing himself to Wagner and Rodin, both of whom 'had to suffer for being "new"' (*CL2*: 418). Conrad brought a Continental inflection to the English novel: his early masters included Flaubert, Maupassant and Anatole France; of the Russians, he claimed to admire only Turgenev. The latter's *Fathers and Sons* (1862), Dostoevsky's *Crime and Punishment* (1866) and Tolstoy's *War and Peace* (1869) would all be published by the time he was in his teens, and would variously influence his own work.

When Conrad began writing, the popular taste was for novels that reflected Britain's imperial outlook. Extending back to the tradition established by Captain Marryat and Robert Louis Stevenson, and often set against an historical backdrop – G. A. Henty's *With Clive in India* (1884) or Erskine Childers' *The Riddle of the Sands* (1903) – these were characteristically boys' adventure stories in which young men, endowed with pluck rather than introspection, reinvented themselves upon foreign shores. (These are the years in which the *Boys' Own Paper* was first published and also saw the founding of the Boy Scouts movement by Robert Baden-Powell.) Catching the public mood of fascination with colonial life and the exotic, the literary successes include Rider Haggard's *King Solomon's Mines* (1885), heralded by its publisher as 'the most amazing story ever written', Rudyard Kipling's *Kim* (1901), and Edgar Rice Burroughs' *Tarzan of the Apes* (1914). In Conrad's fiction, this 'romantic adventure' tradition was forced to encounter alien ways of thinking that not only exposed the hypocrisies of colonialism but, in the process, also raised unsettling questions about the European self-image.

Conrad's transitional status as an author, straddling the late-Victorian and Modern eras, is felicitously supported by the sense of the baton being passed from one generation of writers to the next within the tradition of the English novel. His first novel, *Almayer's Folly*, a colonial reworking of the Bovary theme, was published in 1895, the year of Thomas Hardy's *Jude the Obscure*. Stung by the novel's critical reception – it was dubbed 'Jude the Obscene' in some quarters – the author devoted the rest of his life to writing poetry. In *Jude the Obscure*, Hardy, the literary chronicler of the century's most significant social event, the mass migration of people from the countryside to the cities, identified the pathology of the age as 'the modern vice of unrest' (68). Emigré, economic migrant, immigrant, the contours of Conrad's own life trace this condition. In *Victory* (1915) he speaks of 'the age in which we are camped like bewildered travellers in a garish, unrestful hotel' (3). Nor was Conrad alone in his status as outsider: his fellow instigators of Modernism in English literature include Henry James, Ezra Pound, T. S. Eliot, W. B. Yeats and James Joyce: Americans and Irish. Through their combined influence the national 'English' tradition of literature was forced into correspondence with imported ideas and techniques.

These were explosive years within the arts as writers challenged prevailing standards and orthodoxies of what was deemed 'acceptable'. For instance, at the conclusion of Henrik Ibsen's *A Doll's House* (1879), Nora slams the door on contemporary bourgeois marriage that sustains the entrapment of women – a theme Conrad would adapt for his first story with an English setting, 'The Return', in 1897 and broach again in 'To-morrow' in 1902 – while *Ghosts* (1881) provoked a storm of abuse as it exposed the disturbing underside of social respectability and, by extension, the basis of patriarchy. Bookending the Modernist period in English letters, Robert Louis Stevenson's *The Strange Case of Dr. Jekyll and Mr. Hyde* (1886) and D. H. Lawrence's *Lady Chatterley's Lover* (1928) represent its audacity and iconoclasm, as the focus shifted from the Victorian 'social' novel to modern dramas of alienation. Fittingly, in the age of Freud, literature concentrated increasingly upon representations of individual psychology, developing such techniques as 'stream of consciousness' to mimic the random flux of thought, while simultaneously conveying the self as an exiled sensitivity, in touch with, yet simultaneously detached from, the surrounding world.

Ideologically and technically Conrad's writings reflect the intellectual daring of the age, and helped direct the course of the English novel. In 'Mr. Bennett and Mrs. Brown' ([1924] 1981), Virginia Woolf identified Conrad and Hardy as the two great contemporary English authors from whom the younger generation of writers might learn their craft.

QUESTIONS

1. In what ways can Conrad's life be viewed as a pathology of Modernism?
2. The artistic movement known as Modernism is generally defined as spanning the years 1880 to 1930. What major historical and political events/movements are important to consider in order to understand Modernism?
3. Harold Rosenberg defined Modernism as 'the tradition of the new', Explore the contrast that Modernist texts demonstrate between the opposed terms 'tradition' and 'new'.

CHAPTER 2

LANGUAGE, STYLE AND FORM

CONRAD'S ENGLISH

Reacting to reviews of his great metropolitan novel, *The Secret Agent* (1907), Conrad fulminated: 'I've been so cried up of late as a sort of freak, an amazing bloody foreigner writing in English' (*CL*3: 488). Although he is regarded as one of the great stylists in the language, writing in English meant writing in Conrad's third language, after Polish and French. Naturally sensitive to charges that he was an outsider – charges made more poignant by the fact that he was castigated in some quarters of the Polish press for having turned his back on his native language – he felt compelled to defend his decision to write in 'English – the speech of my secret choice' (*A Personal Record*: 136). Explaining this in the 'Author's Note' to *A Personal Record*, Conrad wrote: 'English was for me neither a matter of choice nor adoption. The merest idea of choice had never entered my head. And as to adoption – well, yes, there was adoption; but it was I who was adopted by the genius of the language, which directly I came out of the stammering stage made me its own so completely that its very idioms I truly believe had a direct action on my temperament and fashioned my still plastic character' (v).

Although Conrad claimed to have had to work 'like a coalminer in his pit quarrying all my English sentences out of a black night', and despaired as late as 1907 that 'English is still for me a foreign language whose handling demands a fearful effort' (*CL*4: 112, *CL*3: 401), his linguistic maturity is even more impressive for being in his third tongue. As a contemporary reviewer of Conrad's second novel, *An Outcast of the Islands* (1896), put it: 'Mr. Conrad's English gets into one's veins' (*CL*1: 277). His grammar, vocabulary and syntax are enriched by this linguistic potpourri, and Gallicisms and Polonisms are part of his style, leading some commentators to find Conrad's English un-English. But Conrad's attitude towards the language was scrupulous, and demonstrates his keen awareness of himself as an exemplar of English prose, attempting to achieve in and with it a sense of precision, clarity and rhythm that is, paradoxically, more French, and perhaps is explicitly part of his inheritance from Flaubert. Writing to Hugh Clifford in 1899 he offers the following advice on the craft of writing: 'The things "as they are" exist in words; therefore words should be handled with care lest the picture, the image of truth abiding in facts, should become distorted – or blurred. ... the *whole* of the truth lies in the presentation; therefore the expression should be studied in the interest of veracity. This is the only morality of *art* apart from *subject*' (*CL*2: 200).

John Conrad remembers how his father did not approve of words being 'made a mess of' and records an incident when, replying to a letter from John's form master, Conrad took the opportunity to point out to him: 'I am surprised that you, along with so many other Englishmen, make the mistake of writing "different to" instead of "different from"' (1981: 101, 176). He was also evidently proud of his contribution to English letters, noting that 'the new generation in France are, according to the publishers, reading my books in English. That is surely a great victory for English!' (in Ray ed., 1990: 211). Conrad recognized that style provided a frame of reception for his stories, declaring himself to be 'haunted, mercilessly haunted by the *necessity* of style' (*CL*2: 50). The meaning of his works resides as much in the words on the page as in the mind of the reader. As he admitted to Clifford in 1902: 'Style is a matter of great concern to me as you know; and perhaps my very anxiety as to the proper use of a language of which I feel myself painfully ignorant produces the effect of laboured construction: whereas as a matter of striving my aim is simplicity and ease' (*CL*2: 460).

In a famous passage from his 'Preface' to *The Nigger of the 'Narcissus'* (1897), often regarded as Conrad's early artistic credo, Conrad summarized his approach to writing in terms that recognize an intrinsic relationship between language and style:

> it is only through an unremitting never-discouraged care for the shape and ring of sentences that an approach can be made to plasticity, to colour, and that the light of magic suggestiveness may be brought to play for an evanescent instant over the commonplace surface of words: of the old, old words, worn thin, defaced by ages of careless usage.
>
> The sincere endeavour to accomplish that creative task, to go as far on that road as his strength will carry him, to go undeterred by faltering, weariness or reproach, is the only valid justification for the worker in prose. And if his conscience is clear, his answer to those who in the fullness of a wisdom which looks for immediate profit, demand specifically to be edified, consoled, amused; who demand to be promptly improved, or encouraged, or frightened, or shocked, or charmed, must run thus: My task which I am trying to achieve is, by the power of the written word to make you hear, to make you feel – it is, before all, to make you *see*. That – and no more, and it is everything. If I succeed, you shall find there according to your deserts: encouragement, consolation, fear, charm – all you demand – and, perhaps, also that glimpse of truth for which you have forgotten to ask. (ix–x)

Formulated as a progression, within which sensory perception (hearing) leads, by way of affective conviction (feeling), to mental insight (seeing), the narrator's task thus involves creating the conditions whereby such insight might be gained by the reader. With its emphasis upon the atmosphere surrounding the tale rather than the details of tale itself, Marlow's storytelling provides an expression of Conrad's poetics. As he asks his audience in *Heart of Darkness*: 'Do you see the story? Do you see anything?' (82).

STYLE

Conrad's style in *Heart of Darkness* is characterized by indirectness. Writing to R. B. Cunninghame Graham on 8 February 1899, Conrad cautioned: 'the idea is so wrapped up in secondary nations that You – even You! – may miss it!' (*CL*2: 157). The emphasis falls upon the suggestive and intangible rather than the descriptive and factual. None the less, when asked where Marlow's adventure occurs, readers generally answer: in the Congo Free State. But this is to blur the boundary between the facts of Conrad's life and the experiences of Marlow, a fictional creation. Apart from the Thames setting for the narration, Conrad deliberately avoids specificity. Even where place names are mentioned, such as 'Gran' Bassam' and 'Little Popo' (61), they seem designed to conjure up the sense of exotic strangeness rather than a geographical reality. In consequence, Marlow's geographical wanderings can be read as metaphors for a narrative of self-discovery. *Heart of Darkness* is a tale not only of Belgian colonialism but more significantly of the colonial enterprise *tout court*, while Marlow's story of his voyage into the unknown can be seen to mimic the imperial impulse itself.

In a famous, early criticism of Conrad's style, F. R. Leavis complained of 'adjectival insistence' (1948: 177). One thinks of Kurtz's 'gift of expression', described as 'the bewildering, the illuminating, the most exalted and most contemptible, the pulsating stream of light, or the deceitful flow from the heart of an impenetrable darkness' (113–14), or his face: 'I saw on that ivory face the expression of sombre pride, of ruthless power, of craven terror – of an intense and hopeless despair' (149). In *Heart of Darkness*, Marlow's style is guided by metaphors that offer invitations to interpretation while never yielding a single meaning. In this manner, style conveys his insecurity when confronted by cultural difference, and, in the process, the correspondence between words and the world they describe is refashioned. Increasingly, Marlow's language is linked not to the world but to his mental state and perceptions of the world. The forest's stillness, for instance, is described as 'the stillness of an implacable force brooding over an inscrutable intention' (93). Definition is sought, and compressed into phrases that are both lyrically resonant and metaphorically ambiguous. The allusiveness creates a productive sense of strangeness, giving the novella a metaphysical dimension. Similarly, as Marlow strains to describe nightmares trapped beneath the patina of respectability, the resulting interplay of concealment and disclosure places the reader at the intersection of narrative and psychological insights.

For all the talk of Conrad's foreignness, his prose is often strikingly poetic in its qualities – such as the sibilance in: 'On silvery sandbanks hippos and alligators sunned themselves side by side' (93) – and marked by sentences that display lyricism and rhythmic balance. Here, for instance, is Marlow's description of the Eldorado Exploring Expedition: 'Their talk, however, was the talk of sordid buccaneers: it was reckless without hardihood, greedy without audacity, and cruel without courage; there was not an atom of foresight or of serious intention in the whole batch of them, and they did not seem aware these things are wanted for the work of the world' (87). The parallel adjectival structure – reckless/hardihood, greedy/audacity, cruel/courage – calls attention to itself: the second adjective in each pair contains more syllables than the first, giving the emphasis to what these adventurers are 'without'. Furthermore, once we remember that this is an oral narrative, the devices of repetition, alliteration and internal rhyme suggest a fine ear for rhetorical persuasion.

Such rhythms in the fine detail are replicated in the overall shape of the narrative where Marlow's narration is bifurcated, to-ing and fro-ing between the unfolding story and his commentary upon its implications. Marlow's self-consciousness as a narrator is evident in the manner in which he struggles to find the right word or phrase to relate his thoughts. During a pause in the narration he says: '. . . No, it is impossible; it is impossible to convey the life-sensation of any given epoch of one's existence – that which makes its truth, its meaning – its subtle and penetrating essence. It is impossible. We live, as we dream – alone ... .' (82). Textually mimicking his own unease at revisiting these memories, the sentences strain for precision, forced back upon themselves through repetition. Much of the suggestive power in Marlow's narrative lies precisely in its quality of indirectness rather than directness, forcing the reader to collaborate by filling in the gaps in order to make sense of the experience.

Even Marlow's relationship with Kurtz is finally formulated in this manner: 'It is his extremity that I seem to have lived through. True, he had made that last stride, he had stepped over the edge, while I had been permitted to draw back my hesitating foot. And perhaps in this is the whole difference; perhaps all the wisdom, and all truth, and all sincerity, are just compressed into that inappreciable moment of time in which we step over the threshold of the invisible. Perhaps!' (151). The first sentence balances the assured opening – 'It is' – against the speculative 'I seem', setting the rhythm for the two sentences that follow: the definite statement in the first – 'True, he had . . . he had' – is subject to qualification and question in the second where the repeated word 'perhaps' is brought into unsettling correspondence with completeness ('all the wisdom . . . all truth . . . all sincerity'). And how should one interpret the exclamatory 'Perhaps!' that follows? Does it undercut the aggrandizement of Kurtz, or wishfully confirm it? Conrad's style in *Heart of Darkness* makes a virtue of vagueness and allusiveness to a degree that necessitates, rather than merely invites, metaphysical interpretation.

To appreciate the manner in which style enacts the process whereby a river journey can acquire the metaphorical prolongations that transform it into an odyssey into the hidden depths of human consciousness, consider this expansive sentence describing the sound of The Intended's voice: ' "It is the gift of the great," she went on, and the sound of her low voice seemed to have the accompaniment of all other low sounds, full of mystery, desolation, and sorrow, I have ever heard – the ripple of the river, the soughing of the trees swayed by the wind, the murmurs of the crowds, the faint ring of incomprehensible words cried from afar, the whisper of a voice speaking from the threshold of an eternal darkness' (159). The accumulation of images invests The Intended's 'low voice' with more and more reference, to the point where it overwhelms the hesitancy of the word 'seemed'. The image-cluster derives recognizably from Marlow's African adventure and leads, like the river journey, to Kurtz, in the final abstract formulation. In other words, the structure of the sentence both enacts the scale of Marlow's adventure and suggests the intangibility of its conclusions.

The power of suggestiveness that characterizes Marlow's storytelling is introduced by the frame narrator who offers this explanation of his storytelling technique: 'The yarns of seamen have a direct simplicity, the whole meaning of which lies within the shell of a cracked nut. But Marlow was not typical (if his propensity to spin yarns be excepted), and to him the meaning of an episode was not inside like a kernel but outside, enveloping the tale which brought it out only as a glow brings out a haze, in the likeness of one of these misty halos that sometimes are made visible by the spectral illumination of moonshine' (48). In her essay, 'Modern Fiction', Virginia Woolf echoes this description when attempting to define the nature of reality that novelists need to capture if they are to truly represent human experience: 'Life is not a series of gig lamps symmetrically arranged; life is a luminous halo, a semi-transparent envelope surrounding us from the beginning of consciousness to the end' (1942: 189). The meaning of the tale thus resides less in the details and more in the atmosphere or impression they evoke, less in what is said than how this is interpreted by his audience. In his letters Conrad repeatedly emphasized the role of the reader in the production of meaning, writing to R. B. Cunninghame Graham, 'one writes only half the book; the other half is with the reader', and to Harriet Mary Capes 'the reader collaborates with the author' (*CL*2: 370; *CL*2: 394).

As the 'gloom' hanging over London, the use of terms like 'haze' and 'misty' to define Marlow's narration, or the mist on the African river all remind the reader, *Heart of Darkness* was written in the great age of Impressionism in the visual arts. It was Claude Monet's *Impression, soleil levant* (Impression, sun rising) of 1872 that gave this artistic movement its name, when a critic sarcastically dubbed the painting 'impressionistic'. Monet famously responded: 'Poor blind idiots. They want to see everything clearly, even through the fog!' (in Renoir, 1962: 157). In literature, this technique manifests itself in the attempt to convey experience by capturing fleeting impressions of reality or mood. Reviewing Conrad's *An Outcast of the Islands* (1896), H. G. Wells described the style as 'like river-mist; for a space things are seen clearly, and then comes a great grey bank of printed matter, page on page, creeping round the reader, swallowing him up' (Sherry, ed., 1973: 73). In a late letter, Conrad described his art as 'fluid, depending on grouping (sequence) which shifts, and on the changing lights giving varied effects of perspective' (*LL*2: 317).

In Marlow's tale, the vague 'brooding' presence of nature contributes to his visionary experience, helping to deepen his character as he projects personal unease onto his surroundings. The reader negotiates the tale through atmosphere and suggestion as Marlow struggles to find appropriate words to describe his increasingly mystical experience. Central to the story's coercive rhythms, the repetition of words like 'brooding' and 'darkness' replicate Marlow's haunting memories in the narrative style. Anticipating this, repetition characterises the novella's opening paragraphs. No matter how the narrator chooses to introduce these paragraphs, whether describing 'The sea-reach of the Thames', 'The Director of Companies', 'the bond of the sea', or the sunset, they invariably conclude with a negative vision of London: 'a mournful gloom, brooding motionless over the biggest, and the greatest, town on earth', 'not out there in the luminous estuary, but behind him, within the brooding gloom', 'the gloom to the west, brooding over the upper reaches', and 'the touch of that gloom brooding over a crowd of men' (45–6). Suggesting the unnamed London as the source of the story's 'brooding gloom', this pattern establishes an ideological, rather then merely a contextual, frame for Marlow's narrative, prompting the suspicion that the human 'darkness' he encounters in Africa is carried there and released by Europeans.

This is a narrative of indirection. It proceeds by analogy, impression and symbolism. Paradoxically, Marlow's compulsion to tell the story is matched by his reluctance to confront its revelations. Concerned with the limits of his comprehension, 'the culminating point of my experience' (51), at its core lie 'unspeakable rites' (118). Nothing is ever merely one thing in this narrative. Africa is mentioned once by name in the text; on a map, inspiration for a schoolboy dream of adventure. Hereafter it is presented less as a place than a state of consciousness. The deeper Marlow travels into the jungle, the less it appears to be simply jungle. Instead, personified as a watchful, patient presence, inimical to the European invasion, it assumes a protean status: objective correlative for his anxious state of mind; symbolic representation of forces by which Kurtz is governed, and of which he is a plaything; a space in which dark human fantasies are realized. Marlow's journey begins with being 'charmed' (53) by the snake-like river; it comes to resemble a nightmarish exploration into the depths of consciousness itself. It can only be told in abstract terms. The story's concern with identity is reflected in the fact that, apart from Marlow and Kurtz, no other character is named in the story. Either they are anonymous 'types', mainly Company functionaries, or they are invested with archetypal significance, like the three women, draped in black, that Marlow meets at the Company offices, symbolically 'guarding the door of Darkness' (57).

MARLOW

The creation of Marlow, the sailor-turned-raconteur, is one of Conrad's great achievements. Marlow is English and so provides Conrad, an immigrant author writing for an English readership, with a recognisable English perspective. Simultaneously character and interpreter, Marlow has a dual narrating presence, recounting the tale and transforming its action into moral and philosophical enquiry. In her obituary of Conrad, written in 1924, Virginia Woolf claimed that 'Conrad was compound of two men; together with the sea captain dwelt that subtle, refined, and fastidious analyst whom he called Marlow' (1942: 285–6). This leads to her 'rough-and-ready distinction' that 'it is Marlow who comments, Conrad who creates' (287). If this seems to strain the distinction between life and art, between the author and the narrator, then Conrad himself encouraged posterity to bracket the man and the work, claiming of *Heart of Darkness*, for example, that it is 'experience pushed a little (and only very little) beyond the actual facts of the case for the perfectly legitimate, I believe, purpose of bringing it home to the minds and bosoms of the readers' ('Author's Note', *Youth*: xi).

Marlow's presence as an English narrator thus weaves Conrad's own life into the life of his adopted nation, through the potent myth of English literature. In Najder's words: 'Thanks to Marlow's duality, Conrad could feel solidarity with, and a sense of belonging to, England by proxy, at the same time maintaining a distance such as one has toward a creation of one's imagination. Thus, Conrad, although he did not permanently resolve his search for a consistent consciousness of self-identity, found an integrating point of view' (1983: 231). Character and narrator, positioned between the tale and the reader, Marlow can be thought of as Janus-faced, seeing and addressing both the colonial 'world' of *Heart of Darkness* and the British 'island' of the reader. Indeed, his attitude towards England (and Empire), now questioning and now reverent, depends upon this dual perspective, enabling the irony that defines his art. Rooted in the late-nineteenth-century marine and colonial worlds, Marlow's tales blend the facts and myths of Empire, yet it is also through Marlow that Great and Greater Britain are brought into critical contiguity and focus.

Even as he mediates between his audience and the fictional world he creates, Marlow's narrative dramatizes the transformative energy of orality: his is storytelling for an audience prepared to listen to the world's voices. His first-person narration combines the intimacy of an 'I' speaking to 'you' with the testament of witnessed experience. Furthermore, while emphasizing Marlow's subjective experience, and tacitly inviting the reader to look beyond the necessarily limited perspective of subjective vision, the narrating situation between Marlow and his audience provides a constant reminder of the transformation of personal into social understanding. Significantly, when introducing Marlow, the frame-narrator distinguishes between his curiosity and the 'stay-at-home' (48) minds of seamen generally.

Typical of first-person narrative, Marlow's style combines the immediacy of witnessed experience with techniques designed to replicate the processes of remembering this experience. Drawing attention to this strategy, Ian Watt (1980) christens it 'delayed decoding', whereby the listener-reader is invited to share in Marlow's experience, understanding – or decoding – unfolding events at the same rate as he does. For example, when the steamboat that he is commanding comes under attack on the journey between the Central and Inner stations, Marlow's first impression is: 'Sticks, little sticks, were flying about – thick: they were whizzing before my nose, dropping below me, striking behind me against my pilot-house' (109). Shortly afterwards this initial impression is revised: 'Arrows, by Jove! We were being shot at!' (110). The confusion is brief, but sufficient to recreate Marlow's own delayed interpretation of the moment. Story and storytelling are intimately connected as delayed decoding elevates the tale's uncertain meaning to the status of a formal principle.

A more sustained example is provided when the steamboat arrives at the Inner Station. Surveying the station through his binoculars, Marlow observes: 'There was no enclosure or fence of any kind; but there had been one apparently, for near the house half-a-dozen slim posts remained in a row, roughly trimmed, and with their upper ends ornamented with round carved balls' (121). The description suggests dereliction: apparent earlier concern for the appearance of the station has been replaced by neglect. But this notion of physical decay is reconfigured as moral dereliction once Marlow returns to the scene with more concentrated vision: 'These round knobs were not ornamental but symbolic; they were expressive and puzzling, striking and disturbing – food for thought and also for the vultures if there had been any looking down from the sky; but at all events for such ants as were industrious enough to ascend the pole. They would have been even more impressive, those heads on stakes, if their faces had not been turned to the house' (130). As in the previous example, delayed revelation about the true nature of the 'ornaments' here ensures that the audience shares Marlow's shock. But, in an extension of the technique, actual decoding is further delayed until its impact upon Marlow has been registered, initially in a sentence laden with his subjective interpretation ('symbolic', 'expressive', 'puzzling', and so on), as he searches for the right word, and references to scavengers. Only then are the ornaments explained, but even when it comes – 'those heads on stakes' – the revelation is presented as an afterthought, with the phrase presented as a right-displaced subject in the sentence. Such attention to Marlow's process of understanding foregrounds the act of interpretation. Casting the facts of the story into the background, Marlow's meditation reminds the reader of the frame-narrator's judgement that 'meaning' is not immanent but 'enveloping the tale' (48).

With its emphasis upon sensation and subjective perception – think of how looking at an Impressionist canvas involves choosing exactly where to stand: stand too close and the effects become blurred – such imprecision forms an integral part of Impressionist meaning. In *Heart of Darkness*, this process might be said to begin with the title. Does 'heart' qualify 'darkness', suggesting its essential quality, or the other way round: is this about dark-heartedness? Furthermore, given the story's setting in the so-called 'Dark Continent' – Stanley's *In Darkest Africa* appeared in 1890 – the title simultaneously connotes the dark interior of the African jungle and this jungle as a representation of human interiority. Symbols and symbolic gestures provide further instances of the proliferation of meaning. For instance, when the frame-narrator introduces Marlow it is in 'the pose of a Buddha preaching in European clothes and without a lotus-flower' (50) – a description returned to in the final paragraph, where he sits 'apart, indistinct and silent, in the pose of a meditating Buddha' (162). While the association casts Marlow's story-telling in a philosophical light, the absence of the symbolic flower has implications for the enlightenment it contains. Does it, perhaps, signal that enlightenment remains elusive in the tale?

As befits a memory-narrative, Marlow's is subject to chronological disruptions, now anticipatory – as in the references to Kurtz's Intended (115) or Kurtz's report for the International Society for the Suppression of Savage Customs (117–18) – and now retrospective: recalling the interview with the Company doctor (72), or Kurtz's final words during the interview with the Intended. These reminders that Marlow knows the whole tale before he starts telling it call attention to the manner of narrating while, subtly and simultaneously, eroding the boundaries between past and present, and, by extension, those between the tale and its reception. Further enhancing the sense of dislocation, Marlow's style is characterized by hesitancy. What are termed 'modalizing locutions' – 'as if', 'like', 'seemed', and so on – punctuate his narrative, allowing him to imply rather than assert. In this manner, Marlow's meditations, connected to and disparate from his experiences, regulate and guide his listeners' responses through inferences that suggest what could be rather than what is, making them better listeners in the process.

FORM

Heart of Darkness is a frame-narrative. Marlow's story of his journey to find Kurtz and its consequences is structurally 'framed' by the presence of an unnamed narrator, who introduces the story and occasionally interjects. This formal arrangement, whereby Conrad writes a novella in which a frame-narrator introduces Marlow, who then tells a story about Kurtz, creates the impression of being taken deeper and deeper into the narrative by a telescoping process, suggesting a quest for essence through the steadily refined focus. But the frame narration is more than a structural device; it also establishes an ideological context for Marlow's tale.

The narrative begins by establishing the setting: Marlow recounts his story to four friends aboard the *Nellie*, a small pleasure boat, moored in the Thames estuary. (This detail has an autobiographical source: Fountaine Hope, one of Conrad's earliest English friends – they met in 1880 – had also been an officer in the merchant service and owned a yawl called the *Nellie* in which he and Conrad enjoyed trips along the Thames estuary. After their honeymoon in Brittany, the Conrads settled in Stanford-le-Hope, in Essex, in order to be near the Hopes, to whom *Lord Jim* is dedicated.) Historicized, this setting, near the mouth of the Thames with London in the background, acquires acute relevance in a story about colonialism. Britain's capital city, London was also the symbolic heart of the British Empire that, by the time of the story's composition, extended to a quarter of the world's population and whose bounty made its way into the warehouses of London's docks. Seen thus, the Thames provides the artery connecting the worlds of Great and Greater Britain.

Besides the frame-narrator, Marlow's audience consists of three men identified only by their social roles: the Director of

Companies, the Accountant and the Lawyer. At first sight their occupations seem merely arbitrary, connoting a certain social standing, but, as the reader quickly discovers, nothing in this novella is irrelevant. These three men, allied by 'the bond of the sea' (45), all have their counterparts in the tale to follow. Prior to his journey, Marlow is interviewed in 'the sepulchral city' by the 'great man himself', carrying away from the encounter 'an impression of pale plumpness in a frock-coat' (56); once in Africa, at the first station he meets the Company's chief accountant with his books 'in apple-pie order' (68); and, more subtly, Marlow notes that the enslaved Africans he sees at this trading station have been brought 'from all the recesses of the coast in all the legality of time contracts' (66). By forcing the story of colonialism into correspondence with its narrative frame, such comparisons will also pose unsettling questions about British colonialism.

The hymn to Britain's maritime history that follows strikes a deceptively Kiplingesque note. Citing the examples of Sir Francis Drake (1540?–96), the first Englishman to circumnavigate the globe, and Sir John Franklin (1786–1847), the Arctic explorer who led an expedition to discover the North-West Passage, a shortcut between Europe and Asia through the waters north of Canada, the sequence initially appears jingoistic. The devil, however, lies in the detail. Drake returned to England with plunder worth some half a million pounds in Elizabethan currency, while Franklin's attempt failed when his ships became icebound and involved cannibalism. The bearing of these two examples upon the story to follow is thus both prescient and stark. This is not to dismiss the glory of the British Empire, but rather to temper it, for the knowing reader, with equivocating claims. Even the civilizing impulse behind global exploration, its adventurers 'bearing the sword, and often the torch' (47), is undermined by the order of presentation: the sword precedes the torch. Most strikingly, the consolatory Victorian truism about the sun's never setting on the British Empire is invoked at the paragraph break: 'The dreams of men, the seeds of commonwealths, the germs of empires. | The sun set' (47). Clearly, the evening setting itself is designed to frame Marlow's narration both literally and metaphorically.

Aboard the *Nellie*, the men listen to Marlow's words while waiting for the tide to turn to begin their cruise. At the conclusion, the Director notices that they 'have lost the first of the ebb' (162). There is no attempt to respond to the story. Instead, recounted between the tides, the tale distracts the men, all former sailors, from the task at hand, symbolically suspending the sailing venture. During the story there are few reminders of the presence of Marlow's audience beyond occasional interruptions to dramatize the telling – such as when Marlow pauses to light his pipe (114) or one of his listeners objects to his turn of phrase: 'Try to be civil, Marlow' (94) – and hints of their reaction: 'It had become so pitch dark that we listeners could hardly see one another. . . . The others might have been asleep, but I was awake' (83). Once we identify Marlow's listeners with the colonial endeavour, this last speculation seems damning, suggesting that they do not want to recognize its dark truths. But what is an adequate response? After all, even before Marlow's account of how he once turned 'fresh-water sailor for a bit', the frame-narrator cautions that we are 'to hear about one of Marlow's inconclusive experiences' (51), suggesting even before it begins that this story has no conclusion. As such, Marlow's perspective serves as criticism of European mores. Dramatizing the insecurity of the narrating self confronted by cultural difference, his is a European perspective unable to colonially appropriate the world.

In *Heart of Darkness*, first-person narrating acquires a characteristically Modernist inflection, portraying Marlow as an exiled sensibility, alienated from his surroundings. As he avers: 'We live, as we dream – alone', and during the tale he is described as 'no more to us than a voice' (82, 83). The fact that his narration begins apparently in mid-thought supports this sense of immediacy: '"And this also," said Marlow suddenly, "has been one of the dark places of the earth"' (48). Like oral storytelling itself, these opening words, containing a Biblical quotation (Psalm 74: 20–21), confer the weight of the distant past upon the tale, much as for a contemporary audience it would have been a phrase frequent in colonialist discourse. Why Marlow tells his tale, however, remains a mystery, leading to the suspicion that, like Coleridge's Ancient Mariner, he is compelled to do so. This is a story that, for all of its unsettling implications about the nature of man, *has* to be told. Echoing the frame-narrative, Marlow's tale of his experiences in Africa is itself 'framed' as he begins it obliquely: first, in his brief opening words, and then in his tale of a Roman legionary serving in ancient Britain at the height of the Roman Empire. While establishing historical parallels between different ages of imperial conquest, these false starts suggest a certain hesitancy to address his experience. Perhaps Marlow is unwilling yet compelled to recount the tale that follows.

Envisioning the 'utter savagery' of Roman Britain as perceived by one of her conquerors, 'a decent young citizen in a toga' (50), Marlow's introductory observations diminish the distance between the historical frame and its late-nineteenth century content. These ideas – including the 'utter savagery' of the natives, together with the 'fascination of the abomination' this exerts on the intruders – will acquire contemporary resonance in the tale of contemporary colonialism. Reinforcing the idea that the meaning of a Marlow tale is to be found in its surrounding atmosphere, this historical parallel also questions the relationship between the story and its frame. Where, for example, does Marlow's story start? Is it in the recent past, when he begins to describe how he secured employment in Africa? Or is it further back, in the contextualizing tale of the Roman Empire, or in the Biblical quotation? That such questions persist is itself a comment upon the impossibility of a 'frame' containing, and so defining the limitations of, this story, and prefigures a tale whose implications extend beyond the occasion of its telling. As Samuel Beckett wittily commented on the relationship between form and content in Marcel Proust's *A la recherche du temps perdu* (1913–27): 'The whisky bears a grudge against the decanter' (1965: 21–2).

A practical instance of this is suggested by the juxtaposed images of the Thames and the map of Africa he describes: the frame-narrator notes that, on the water, 'Flames glided in the river, small green flames, red flames, white flames, pursuing, overtaking, joining, crossing each other – then separating slowly or hastily' (51); Marlow remarks of the map of Africa that 'There was a vast amount of red – good to see at any time, because one knows that some real work is done in there, a deuce of a lot of blue, a little green, smears of orange, and, on the East Coast, a purple patch, to show where the jolly pioneers of progress drink the jolly lager-beer' (55). Like the Romans anecdote, this technical strategy, like a cinematic dissolve, connects the 'traffic of the great city' (51) with the scramble for Africa by European powers, and, by collapsing the distance between them, further identifies events in the tale with the moment of their reception. Marlow's narrative gestures both backwards – through the historical frame which, among other things, suggests something intrinsic in the human condition while providing a tacit reminder that empires are transient – and forwards, through its reception: first, by the fictional audience aboard the *Nellie*; then, by Conrad's contemporary readership, for whom Empire was the great fact of the age; and, then, across a century of readers and critics who continue to be lured by the fascination exerted by this tale of moral and cultural disintegration.

The structure of Marlow's tale conforms to the traditional quest-narrative that stretches as far back as *The Odyssey*. This invites correspondence with other quests: Marlow's journey into the wilderness is figured as a descent into the underworld – following in the footsteps of Odysseus, Aeneas and Dante – where he meets Kurtz, a latter-day Faust who has sold his soul for forbidden knowledge and power. But this particular quest is a voyage of self-discovery, less a case of Marlow proving himself – as, say, Jason does in Greek mythology – than of his coming to understand something of who he is and, in the process, the limitations of self. In fact, the narrative contains two journeys: the literal upriver venture to find Kurtz, and Marlow's odyssey of self-discovery. He describes his ordeal as 'the farthest point of navigation and the culminating point of my experience' (51). Superimposed upon the facts of the actual voyage, Marlow's commentary on his progress, now personal, now philosophical, offers what Henry James, referring to a later Marlow-narrative, *Chance* (1914), called 'a prolonged hovering flight of the subjective over the outstretched ground of the case exposed' (1984: 149). The African setting provides a realm where Marlow's imagination can wander freely, with its twists and turns replicated in the quest for Kurtz. As such, the two journeys, the telling and the tale, become symbolic representations of each other.

With its emphasis upon the suggestive and intangible, rather than the descriptive and factual, and its insistence upon individualism, symbolism provides the perfect medium for a narrative characterized by openness and deviation. Marlow begins his tale in 'Youth', told to the same audience, by observing: 'You fellows know there are those voyages that seem ordered for the illustration of life, that might stand for a symbol of existence' ('Youth': 3–4). Meditative and philosophical in mood and tone, richly allusive in style, *Heart of Darkness* is similarly 'ordered', to provide an unsettling 'symbol of existence'.

QUESTIONS

1. Critically examine the various consequences of the use of 'frame narration' in *Heart of Darkness*.
2. *Heart of Darkness* is a first-person narrative. What are the advantages and disadvantages of this narrative technique?
3. Identify and illustrate the hallmarks of Conrad's style in *Heart of Darkness*, and discuss how these contribute to the novella's meaning.

CHAPTER 3

READING *HEART OF DARKNESS*

CONRAD'S CONGO

Joseph Conrad spent six months in the Congo Free State, from June to December 1890, as an employee of the Société Anonyme Belge pour le Commerce du Haut-Congo, based in Brussels. He was employed for three years, to replace a riverboat captain named Johannes Freiesleben, commanding a steamboat on the Congo River between Stanley Pool (Kinshasa) and Stanleyville (Kisangani). Upon arriving, Conrad found his steamer damaged and so continued upriver with the Danish master of the *Roi des Belges*. His command of the steamer lasted just ten days, on the return voyage when the captain became too ill to continue his duties. Conrad himself became so ill that he had to be carried most of the 200 miles from Kinshasa to Matadi. His single journey up the Congo River ruined his health and he was invalided home to London, left with a legacy of physical ailments, the after-effects of dysentery and malaria, that would plague him for the rest of his life.

Conrad recorded his immediate impressions of Africa in the two notebooks of his *Congo Diary*. Thanks to these and subsequent research, such as Norman Sherry's *Conrad's Western World* (1971), it is possible to trace correlations between Conrad's travels in Africa and Marlow's journey in *Heart of Darkness*. Thus, 'the seat of government' (62) at which Marlow arrives corresponds to Boma; the first Company Station to Matadi, where, Conrad's *Congo Diary* records, he arrived on 13

June 1890 and there 'Made the acquaintance of Mr. Roger Casement, which I should consider as a great pleasure under any circumstances and now it becomes a positive piece of luck' (1978: 7); the Central Station to Kinshasa; and Kurtz's Inner Station to Kisangani.

But readers must tread warily. These are factual details and do not occur anywhere in *Heart of Darkness*. A work of fiction, the text is deliberately subtle, avoiding explicit placement. It simply doesn't matter to the novella or its meaning exactly where the action is set, aside from a place designated 'yellow' (56) on a map of Africa. To insist upon specific identification, such as the Congo Free State, is to limit the statement Conrad makes. For the same reason, while the novella covertly attacks Belgian imperialism, it is not 'about' that. Such identification is the consequence of scholarship that has traced Conrad's sources, and while these impinge upon the meaning, they are not the meaning itself, which pertains to the self destroyed.

In *Heart of Darkness*, Marlow's narrative is presented in three stages: the first charts his journey from London to the Central Station; the second that from the Central Station to the Inner Station; and the third his meeting with Kurtz and its consequences. This chapter follows these divisions.

PART I: FROM EUROPE TO THE CENTRAL STATION

Literal and psychological 'navigation' are intimately linked in Marlow's narrative from the outset. Supporting the frame-narrator's belief that 'we were fated, before the ebb began to run, to hear about one of Marlow's inconclusive experiences', the beginnings of Marlow's story about the time when he turned 'fresh-water sailor' promise a transformative tale of extreme experience, couched in imprecision: 'It was the farthest point of navigation and the culminating point of my experience. It seemed somehow to throw a kind of light on everything about me – and into my thoughts' (51).

Marlow recalls how his employment in an unnamed African country resulted from his inability to secure a berth in an ocean-going ship. From the outset, his turn of phrase anticipates the clichés of colonialism that will be scrutinized in the narrative. Between ships and 'invading' the homes of his friends, 'as though I had got a heavenly mission to civilize you' (52), he recalls his youthful 'passion for maps', and the ambitions they fostered: 'When I grow up I will go there' (52). In particular, he remembers how a mighty river in central Africa 'fascinated me as a snake would a bird' (52). Neither the Congo nor the Congo River is ever named in *Heart of Darkness*, although there are sufficient clues for the reader to be able to identify them. Two consequences follow from this: first, the Congo provides an image of colonialism generally; and, secondly, the reader is conjoined in Marlow's 'fascination' and made to take an interpretive share in his 'navigation'. The image of the river as a snake invites obvious comparisons with the serpent in the Garden of Eden, and, with it, casts the story as a retelling of the quest for knowledge that entailed the fall of man. This is the first of a number of potential mythical readings of this story, whose multiform nature lends it the qualities of a parable, reinforced by Marlow's beginning, in the fashion of the preacher, with a Biblical quotation: 'And this also . . . has been one of the dark places of the earth' (48).

Since Marlow's boyhood aspirations the representation of Africa on maps has undergone a transformation: formerly 'a blank space of delightful mystery', the continent has been 'filled . . . with rivers and lakes and names', but, paradoxically, the work of explorers has rendered it 'a place of darkness' (52). However consonant with contemporary designations of Africa as 'the dark continent', this progression inverts the traditional association of knowledge with light, and in the process subtly suggests that European involvement in Africa (and by extension in colonialism anywhere) is responsible for darkness rather than enlightenment. This logical inversion extends to morality in the tale of Fresleven. Remembering the existence of a Continental concern that trades on the river, Marlow solicits the assistance of his aunt who has some influence with the administration, to help him secure employment, taking charge of one of the company's steamboats. Her efforts prove successful, and Marlow is appointed to replace a Danish steamboat-captain, Fresleven, killed by the natives after a cultural misunderstanding.

These fictional incidents have their basis in fact: Conrad was assisted by his 'aunt' (in fact, a marriage relation), Marguerite Poradowska, resident in Brussels, in his efforts to gain employment in the Congo, although the extent of her influence remains uncertain; and his predecessor, Captain Johannes Freiesleben, a Dane, was indeed killed by natives on 29 January 1890 at Tchumbiri (see Sherry 1971: 15–22). While the anecdote conveys something of the dangers of Marlow's venture, the account of Fresleven's death, and of Marlow finding his remains, provides a brief anticipatory insight into the moral state of affairs in the colony. The 'gentlest, quietest creature that ever walked on two legs', Fresleven, believing himself wronged over a bargain involving two hens, 'mercilessly' beat a village chief with a stick – for which he was speared by the chief's son (54). Most significant is the response of the villagers: 'expecting all kinds of calamities' (54), they abandon their homes and flee into the forest. The incident – 'this glorious affair', in Marlow's ironic phrase – is symptomatic of the, equally ironic, 'noble cause' of European involvement in Africa and sets the tone for the fable of unease and disenchantment under the ostensibly ideal surface to follow.

Marlow's account of his interview in the 'city that always makes me think of a whited sepulchre' (55) (that is, Brussels, if one goes back to the story's sources, but the Biblical allusion is richer than 'Brussels', conveying mystery and indirection), resonates with symbolic significance, helping to invest his adventure with mythical prolongations. He himself senses 'something ominous in the atmosphere . . . something not quite right' (56). Like the river journey to follow, his meeting with the 'great man himself' is completed in stages: the outer room, the waiting room, and the 'sanctuary' correspond to the trading stations that will mark his progress on the Congo. In the first room, he encounters two women, 'one fat and the other slim . . . knitting black wool' (55); in the second a white-haired secretary 'wearing a compassionate expression', who beckons to him with 'a skinny forefinger' when it is time for his interview of 'about forty-five seconds' (56). The elder of the two knitters, especially, with a wart on her cheek and a cat on her lap, seems designed to conjure up images of the stereotypical fairy-tale witch. (The epigraph to

Youth is a quotation from Grimm's *Tales*.) But the knitters also recall the Parcae or Fates of Greek mythology. These three sisters presided over the birth and life of humankind: one determining the moment of birth, one spinning out the events of life, and one, Atropos, the eldest, cutting the thread of life. With her glance of 'indifferent placidity' and 'unconcerned wisdom', the older knitter strikes Marlow as 'uncanny and fateful' (56–7). In Africa, he will recall the two knitters as 'guarding the door of Darkness, knitting black wool as for a warm pall', giving added poignancy to his final comment on them, which, invoking the gladiators' salute to Caesar, enhances the classical context of this scene: '*Ave!* Old knitter of black wool. *Morituri te salutant*. Not many of those she looked at ever saw her again – not half, by a long way' (57).

Marlow's brief interview, the reason for his being in 'the sepulchral city', is all but glossed over as attention focuses upon these women. But the impression he carries away is both derisory – 'pale plumpness in a frock-coat' – and countervailing: 'He was five feet six, I should judge, and had his grip on the handle-end of ever so many millions' (56). The inverse relationship between physical size and material power here, itself providing a comment upon the extent of the Company's influence in Africa, will be reformulated when Marlow meets Kurtz, whose name, meaning 'short', is visually contradicted by his height. There follows a visit to the Company doctor, accompanied by a clerk who, while glorifying the Company's business, has no intention of going to Africa. Instead he answers Marlow's question in terms that extend the classical frame of reference: 'I am not such a fool as I look, quoth Plato to his disciples' (57). Extending the contrast between appearance and reality, this 'sententious' response pits wisdom against the folly of going to the Congo, imbuing the venture with an element of madness while, simultaneously, revealing the expedience that underpins it. The Company is doubly parasitic, preying both upon its employees and the Africans in the pursuit of profit. Furthermore, this phrase seems less an actual Platonic quotation than false coin, with symbolic potential: it is fraudulent 'knowledge', and thus extends the deception associated with the Company.

The association of going to Africa with madness is given a further twist when the perfunctory medical examination concludes with the doctor measuring the size of Marlow's skull 'in the interests of science' since, as he says, 'the changes take place inside' (58). Recalling this experience later in the narrative, Marlow will describe himself as 'becoming scientifically interesting' (72). When asked, the doctor admits to being something of an 'alienist', a mental pathologist, viewing his study of those who venture to Africa as part of the advantage the mother country will reap from 'the possession of such a magnificent dependency' (58). None the less, his practice of cranial measurement is symptomatic of nineteenth-century pseudoscience, of the type popularized by criminologists like the Italian Cesare Lombroso (1836–1909), who believed that moral qualities could be 'read' in human appearance. Inevitably, such ideas played into the hands of supremacists, repeatedly identifying 'criminal degenerates' in terms of non-European features. More immediately, the visit to the doctor aligns the African narrative with psychological experience.

Marlow's final duty before leaving Europe is to bid farewell to his aunt, through whom the popular perception – and vindication – of the colonial venture is voiced: 'weaning those ignorant millions from their horrid ways' (59). Their meeting, over a cup of tea by the fireside in her drawing room, seems designed to set up the cosiness of European bourgeois respectability as a foil for the brute reality of its extension into Africa. She thus voices the popular vindication of colonialism, the sentimental alibi behind the 'philanthropic pretence' Marlow discovers. The scramble for Africa was motivated by the '3 Cs' of Christianity, civilization and commerce, the last being vindicated by its conjunction with the other two. The German chancellor Bismarck, for instance, voiced these ideals at the Berlin 'West Africa Conference' of 1884.

Marlow discovers that, when pressing his application for employment, his aunt cast him as 'an exceptional and gifted creature . . . one of the Workers . . . Something like an emissary of light, something like a lower sort of apostle' (59). Such exaggeration points up the scale of wilful self-deception, and Marlow recognizes the clichés for what they are, echoes of the 'rot let loose in print' in contemporary newspapers. But the rhetoric, that obscures rather than describes reality, cannot simply be dismissed: Kurtz will be described in comparable terms. Marlow departs with the impression that 'instead of going to the centre of a continent, I were about to set off for the centre of the earth' (60).

The outward voyage, from Europe to Africa, is made in a French steamer, reminding the reader that French is the language that would have been spoken by most of the Europeans Marlow meets in the (unnamed) Congo, and thus that most of the conversations in *Heart of Darkness*, are translations, sometimes peppered with Gallicisms to give *couleur locale*. One recalls that, at his interview, Marlow had to satisfy the 'great man' as to his command of French. As she sails down the African coast, thereby quickly identifying the nature of European involvement in Africa, the ship makes frequent stops, landing custom-house officers 'to levy toll in what looked like a God-forsaken wilderness' and soldiers 'to take care of the custom-house clerks, presumably' (60) – some of whom, apparently, drown in the surf before ever reaching the shore.

Watching the monotonous African coastline, fringed by 'a colossal jungle, so dark-green as to be almost black' (60), Marlow's adventure takes on an increasingly unreal hue. Names of trading posts, like Gran' Bassam and Little Popo, 'seemed to belong to some sordid farce acted in front of a sinister backcloth', while his idleness and isolation 'seemed to keep me away from the truth of things, within the toil of a mournful and senseless delusion' (60). The use of the modalizing 'seemed' in both of these examples replicates his sense of alienation, as linguistic attempts to describe his situation stray into imprecision. Instead, it is left to the Africans themselves, seen occasionally, who 'wanted no excuse for being there', to provide 'a momentary contact with reality' (61). Marlow's description of these 'black fellows' combines respect for their actuality – 'bone, muscle, a wild vitality, an intense energy of movement, that was as natural and true as the surf along their coast' (61) – with estrangement: 'they had faces like grotesque masks' (61). This conflicted vision establishes the tone that will characterize Marlow's presentation of Africans in the novella. On the one hand, his sympathies set him apart from the Europeans, while, on the other, his racial descriptions are stereotypically of his time. In this manner, Marlow's is simultaneously a transcendent and an authentic voice of his age.

No sooner does the African presence provide Marlow with a sense of belonging to the 'world of straight-forward facts' than the Europeans 'scare it away' (61). The encounter with the French man-of-war, to whom they deliver mail and aboard which fever is killing the men at the rate of three per day, is tinged with absurdity. Anchored off the coast and engaged in hostilities with an unseen enemy, she is described as 'incomprehensible, firing into a continent' (62). Before Marlow even sets foot in Africa, the European presence there is identified as both unwelcome and ridiculous. The reference to fever reminds one that the disease-ridden coast of West Africa was long thought of as the 'White Man's Grave', with Europeans succumbing to malaria and yellow fever. According to Mary Kingsley, an intrepid contemporary traveller in the Congo, 'there is no other region in the world that can match West Africa for the steady kill, kill, kill that its malaria works on the white men who come under its influence' (1897: 681). Perhaps articulating European fears, and hence Marlow's European perspective, the 'wild vitality' of the Africans is quickly drowned out in a chorus of death-centred references: before he arrives at the mouth of the river, the coastal trading stations have become places where 'the merry dance of death and trade goes on in a still and earthy atmosphere as of an overheated catacomb'; the rivers 'streams of death in life'; and the mangroves 'contorted' and writhing in 'the extremity of impotent despair' (62). Unsurprisingly, even before Marlow arrives at his destination, his impression is that 'It was like a weary pilgrimage amongst hints for nightmares' (62). These nightmares quickly acquire concrete definition.

Marlow's voyage ends, after some thirty days, at 'the seat of government', at the mouth of the river. But as his work 'would not begin till some two hundred miles farther on' (62) he quickly sets out for the Company's station, in a steamboat piloted by a Swede. At once a comment upon Marlow's diligence, the speed with which the governmental seat is abandoned for the first of the Company's stations also subtly foregrounds the latter over the former, and hence material interests over the rule of law. The Swedish captain, who speaks to Marlow in English, distinguishes between those who work at the mouth of the river – 'It is funny what some people will do for a few francs a month' – and those who venture further inland: 'I wonder what happens to that kind when it goes up country' (63). And when Marlow announces that he is bound for the interior, the captain retails the recent suicide of a fellow Swede, reminding the reader of Marlow's observation of the old knitter in the Company's offices: 'Not many of those she looked at ever saw her again' (57).

Thirty miles upriver, the Company station gives concrete form to Marlow's 'nightmares'. Against the background noise of the rapids on the river – to circumvent which, the next stage of his journey, ten days later, will be on foot – and detonations caused by attempts to build a railway, Marlow's first impressions of 'the great cause' are brutal. From the vantage point of the steamer he watches people, 'mostly black and naked', moving about 'like ants' (63). The reductive scale subordinates human beings to the work of the Company and dehumanizes them in the process. An air of dereliction hangs over the station. Imports from Europe are everywhere, but these vestiges of distant civilization are marked by their redundancy: a boiler 'wallows' in the grass; an undersized railway truck lies on its back, looking like 'the carcass of some animal'; machinery is left 'decaying'; imported drainage-pipes for the settlement are all broken (63–4). Emblematically, this widespread 'smash-up', a typical 'machine in the jungle' image, points up the negligence and inefficiency of the colonists; more ominously it suggests that vestiges of European civilization lose their meaning and utility once translated into another sphere. Thus, while drainage-pipes, for instance, have their place within a European cultural context, as signifiers of that social progress that depends upon technological sophistication, they are rendered redundant when displaced into a non-European context. The juxtaposition of this material dereliction alongside the treatment of the Africans Marlow witnesses at the station is damning, revealing that neither do European moral values translate to an alternative sphere.

Marlow encounters a chain gang, of six 'criminals', who pass 'with that complete, deathlike indifference of unhappy savages' (64). Set against the aural backdrop of 'objectless blasting' that recalls the French gunboat firing into the continent, the death-in-life impression is traceable to its European source. While the prominent ribs and joints of the Africans tell their own story, the ends of their loincloths that waggle 'like tails' suggest the dehumanizing treatment to which they are subjected. *Heart of Darkness*, is famous, in part, for its macabre historical context. Estimates vary, but some put the figure of Africans who died under Leopold II's reign at ten million. Designed to convey his shock at discovering the truth about Africa, Marlow's narrative is composed of personal impressions that draw some of their force from such statistics. The use of derogatory racial terms like 'savage' jars even as it reminds us that such was the currency of the age. Increasingly, the effect of Marlow's examples is to render unsustainable the glib designation of 'us' as civilized and 'them' as savage. The personal voyage upon which Marlow has embarked is one of disenchantment, from which late-nineteenth-century racial views of culture would not return.

Even the fact that the chain gang is under the command of 'one of the reclaimed' has its historical precedent. The notorious *Force publique* was composed of black mercenaries under white command, so, strictly speaking, many of the atrocities perpetrated were done by 'them' rather than 'us'. The European invasion of Africa is repeatedly presented in extreme and absurd terms, but apart from Marlow, it is not the Europeans who view it thus. Instead, this exaggeration serves to recreate the perspective of the natives, aligning the narrative's sympathies with the colonized rather than the colonizer. However, for all of the corrosive irony in the description, Marlow recognizes that he, too, is identified with 'the great cause of these high and just proceedings' (65).

Confronted by the brutal truth of 'the great cause', Marlow encodes his experiences of human excess, past, present and future, in terms of an infernal taxonomy:

> I've seen the devil of violence, and the devil of greed, and the devil of hot desire; but, by all the stars! These were strong,

> lusty, red-eyed devils, that swayed and drove men – men, I tell you. But as I stood on this hillside, I foresaw that in the blinding sunshine of that land I would become acquainted with a flabby, pretending, weak-eyed devil of a rapacious and pitiless folly. How insidious he could be, too, I was only to find out several months later and a thousand miles farther. (65)

The upriver voyage is thus cast as a journey into humankind's diabolic potential, and acquires immediate force when, attempting to evade the chain gang, Marlow steps into the shade, only to find himself in 'the gloomy circle of some Inferno' where exhausted and discarded Africans, 'nothing early now', and described as 'moribund shapes' and 'bundles of acute angles' (66, 67), have been denuded of their humanity and simply left to die. The sight of men reduced to 'creatures' unable to move except 'on all-fours' renders Marlow 'horror-struck' (67), and would not be out of place in the nightmarish world of Hieronymus Bosch's paintings: 'Black shapes . . . clinging to the earth, half coming out, half effaced within the dim light, in all the attitudes of pain, abandonment, and despair'; 'black shadows of disease and starvation' (66). A further, proleptic, analogy would be to Picasso's *Guernica*, where the forms are geometric, malshaped, 'modern'.

With its deliberate echo of Dante's *Divine Comedy*, the 'grove of death' (70) sequence extends the classical frame of reference, providing a contemporary vision of Hades, with Marlow's entering the shade figured as a descent into a man-made Hell. Furthermore, the designation of the living-dead Africans as 'black shadows' (66) provides an irresistible challenge to the light–dark opposition that provides Europeans with a vindication for colonialism, viewed as bringing enlightenment to a 'savage' darkness for the benefit of those incapable of finding it for themselves. Reduced to 'shadows', a traditional description of the dead, these 'phantoms' (67) increasingly represent not an immanent darkness to be found in Africa but rather the darkness visited upon them by Europe. In effect, the condition of the Africans provides a mirror of European morality, and the guiding metaphors of light and darkness are rendered untenable. As the light/darkness contrast demonstrates, we inhabit a world of symbols and symbolic associations. In *Heart of Darkness*, these symbols are set within the historical conditions necessary to interpret and understand them and, in the process, reformulated.

To one of the Africans he sees, whose 'sunken eyes looked up at me, enormous and vacant, a kind of blind, white flicker in the depths of the orbs, which died out slowly', Marlow gives a ship's biscuit. This simple action separates Marlow from his fellow Europeans, who sap the vitality and, ultimately, life itself from the Africans, but it also suggests the ineffectuality of one voice of sympathy amid exploitation on a grand scale. The African wears 'a bit of white worsted' around his neck. Emblematic of trade, Marlow is unable to fathom the meaning behind this adornment: 'Was it a badge – an ornament – a charm – a propitiatory act?' (67). While the attempt, even if a failed one, at understanding, of searching for meaning, foregrounds Marlow's incomprehension, the interpretive possibilities contained in the sequence, from 'badge' to 'propitiatory act', also enact a transfer from identification and self-proclamation to subservience and appeasement.

Escaping from this nightmarish 'picture of a massacre or a pestilence', Marlow encounters the Company's chief accountant, 'a sort of vision' (67) in his own right. Immaculately clad, having trained one of the native women to do his laundry, and 'devoted to his books, which were in apple-pie order', The Accountant presents a stark contrast to both the 'demoralization of the land' and the 'muddle' typifying the station. Significantly, it is at this point that the true purpose of the European presence is identified: the 'precious trickle of ivory' that comes out of the Interior in return for trade goods, 'rubbishy cottons, beads, and brass-wire' (68). The European concern with booty, with ends rather than means, is signalled within the narrative by an absence: no elephants, dead or alive, are mentioned, even though their commodified form as ivory dominates the tale. In his diary for 24 June 1890, Conrad records: 'Have been myself packing ivory in casks. Idiotic employment' (1978: 7). By the time that *Heart of Darkness*, was published a decade later, rubber rather than ivory attracted Europeans to the country, at the dawn of the age of the motor car. Ominously, Marlow now first hears of Kurtz, 'the man who is so indissolubly connected with my memories of that time' (68). The order of presentation is acute, identifying Kurtz with ivory. According to The Accountant, Kurtz is 'a first-class agent' and 'a very remarkable person', who 'Sends in as much ivory as all the others put together' (69). These comments acquire added impact not only because of who reports them but also in opposition to the station's confusion, signalled by the chaos surrounding the arrival of trading caravans and the presence of a dying agent, lying in the office, a reminder that conditions in Africa are inimical to the Europeans and perhaps suggesting that Nature herself resists their presence.

As an indicator of the self-serving mentality and in-fighting among the Europeans, The Accountant entrusts Marlow with a verbal message for Kurtz – 'that everything here . . . is very satisfactory' – which he is loath to commit to paper because 'you never know who will get hold of your letter – at the Central Station' (70). Nor is The Accountant above self-interest, for he adds his belief that Kurtz is destined to 'go far, very far' in the Company, including himself among of those who, like The Harlequin, are mesmerized by Kurtz, who becomes a sort of fetish for the Europeans.

Marlow glosses over his fifteen-day journey to the Central Station, 'a two-hundred-mile tramp' overland with a caravan of sixty men, beginning with the disclaimer: 'No use telling you about that' (70). Conrad left Matadi on 28 June 1890 and occasional details of his trek to Kinshasa are recorded in the diary he kept at the time. The final entry in the *Congo Diary* is dated 1 August 1890, before Conrad had reached his destination. Marlow sees destroyed and deserted villages, their populations having fled. Turning the tables, he suggests that a comparable invasion, by 'mysterious niggers armed with all kinds of fearful weapons', on the road between Deal and Gravesend, would similarly clear 'every home and cottage' (70). Mischievously, the force of Marlow's domestic/domesticating analogy lies in its capacity to present the natives' view of the European invasion of Africa. By way of illustrative example, he encounters a white man, who claims to be 'looking after the road', with his armed escort of 'lank Zanzibaris', all drunk – Marlow can see neither road not upkeep, 'unless the body of a middle-aged negro, with a bullet-hole in the forehead' (71) he meets three miles further on. One of the most extraordinary things about *Heart of Darkness*, is the degree to which it draws upon fact and upon Conrad's experience, transmuting them both. The horrors Marlow encounters are what Conrad encountered. For instance, his diary of the overland march includes such references as: 'saw at a camp[in]g place the dead body of a Backongo. Shot? Horrid smell'; 'Saw another dead body lying by the path in an attitude of meditative repose'; and 'On the road today passed a skeleton tied up to a post' (1978: 8, 9, 13).

During his employment in the Congo, Conrad was already writing his first novel, *Almayer's Folly* (1895), drawing upon his memories of trading in the Malay Archipelago. It is possible that he kept his somewhat factual and terse diary for similar future creative use. As interesting as the factual correspondences between *Heart of Darkness* and the *Congo Diary* are the deviations. Marlow travels through a devastated landscape; Conrad records passing through villages and marketplaces, and stopping at campsites and mission stations. In the novella, the depopulated countryside provides a further example of hostile European presence while also refining Marlow's narrative focus: his real concern is the effect of Africa on the European self. In his story 'Karain' (1898), Conrad refers to 'the strong life of white men, which rolls on irresistible and hard on the edge of outer darkness' (*Tales of Unrest*: 26). In *Heart of Darkness*, his concern is what happens once white men go over this 'edge'.

But if Marlow does not actually see the natives, and the countryside through which he passes is barely mentioned, their presence is recorded in the occasional 'tremor of far-off drums, sinking, swelling, a tremor vast, faint; a sound weird, appealing, suggestive, and wild – and perhaps with as profound a meaning as the sound of bells in a Christian country' (71). Once again, the sequence of descriptors communicates a multiplicity of perspectives while emphasizing Marlow's rhetorical commitment. By forcing two worlds into comparison, the final speculation also undermines further the distinction between 'us' and 'them', Europeans and Africans, upon which the colonial ideal rests and which will undergo further revision as the narrative develops.

Marlow's first view of the Central Station, set on a 'back water' bordered by 'smelly mud', is sufficient to confirm his view that 'the flabby devil was running the show' (72). White men stroll about 'aimlessly', with long staves in their hands, 'like a lot of faithless pilgrims bewitched inside a rotten fence' (76). The 'deplorable state' of the station, run by a manager who 'inspired uneasiness' (73), is quickly brought home to Marlow: symptomatic of the state of affairs he had discovered at the first station, his steamship lies at the bottom of the river, having been sunk two days before his arrival, in The Manager's 'sudden hurry' to go upriver. During his first interview with The Manager, Marlow finds him 'commonplace in complexion, in feature, in manners, and in voice . . . a common trader . . . nothing more' (73). Conrad's own impressions were no less scathing, writing to Marguerite Poradowska from Kinshasa on 26 September 1890: 'Everything here is repellent to me. Men and things, but men above all', and describing the manager as 'a common ivory dealer with base instincts who considers himself a merchant although he is only a kind of African shop-keeper' (*CL*1: 62). Marlow's progressive disillusionment offers a contrary rhythm to the proclaimed enlightenment of colonialism – or enlightenment of a grim sort.

Suspecting an intrigue, but never certain – 'I fancy I see it now, but I am not sure' (72) – Marlow learns that The Manager had undertaken the upriver expedition, 'in charge of some volunteer skipper' (73), out of a combination of duty – 'The up-river stations had to be relieved' – uncertainty – 'he did not know who was dead and who was alive, and how they got on' – and rumours 'that a very important station was in jeopardy, and its chief, Mr. Kurtz, was ill' (75). Echoing The Accountant of the first station, The Manager describes Kurtz as 'an exceptional man, of the greatest importance to the Company' (75). From such anticipatory comments will spring Marlow's increased fascination with Kurtz, the reason for his mission upriver. What marks The Manager out, as Marlow notes, is his constitution: the fact that he 'was never ill' has enabled him to serve three terms of three years each in Africa. (Conrad feared that it was 'scarcely probable' that he would see his own three-year term through, and in the event served only six months before returning to Europe, severely ill, psychologically and physically. The physical illness would dog him for the rest of his life.) The Manager's belief, that 'Men who come out here should have no entrails' (74), has both physiological and moral connotations. Fittingly, The Brickmaker, who is reputed to be The Manager's spy, is regarded by Marlow as a 'papier-maché Mephistopheles' (80).

It is during his conversation with The Brickmaker, who has been waiting for more than a year for 'something, I don't know what – straw maybe' (77) in order to begin making bricks, that Marlow sees Kurtz's painting: 'a small sketch in oils, on a panel, representing a woman, draped and blindfolded, carrying a lighted torch. The background was sombre – almost black' (79). The iconography in Kurtz's sketch – which summons up the image of *Hope* (1885), painted by G. F. Watts (1817–1904), in which a blindfold female figure sits playing a broken lyre – can be seen as providing a commentary upon the colonial venture, where whatever light is being carried into the darkness is obscured. To Marlow, 'It was just robbery with violence, aggravated murder on a great scale, and men going at it blind' (50).

Like the word 'ivory' – which 'was whispered, was sighed. You would think they were praying to it' (76) – Kurtz's name and reputation obsess the pilgrims: to The Brickmaker, he is 'a prodigy . . . an emissary of science and progress, and devil knows what else . . . a special being' sent to Africa to bring 'higher intelligence, wide sympathies, a singleness of purpose' to the 'cause' (79). Rumours about Kurtz's inevitable advancement within the Company administration exercise the pilgrims, and feed the conspiratorial 'air of plotting' that hangs over the station.

Marlow judges the pilgrims to be motivated by 'imbecile rapacity' behind a 'philanthropic presence' (76, 78). When a grass shed full of trading goods, 'calico, cotton prints, beads, and I don't know what else' (76), catches fire one evening, the pilgrims' response is simultaneously absurdly inadequate and brutal: one gathers a quart of water in a leaking pail, while the 'nigger' identified as the perpetrator is beaten to the point where, after several days trying to recover, he leaves the station 'and the wilderness without a sound took him into its bosom again' (77). It is during his months at the Central Station that the surrounding wilderness begins to assert itself in Marlow's consciousness. Increasingly, descriptions of it punctuate the narrative, to the point where it assumes the status of an indefinable, inimical presence: 'something great and invincible, like evil or truth, waiting patiently for the passing away of this fantastic invasion' (76). The primeval forest is 'spectral' in the moonlight, while the 'silence of the land went home to one's heart' (80). Marlow struggles for precision – the landscape is 'great, expectant, mute' (81) – and surrenders to atmosphere as the already forbidding, particularized setting acquires symbolic depth, accruing meaning as the narrative develops:

> I wondered whether the stillness on the face of the immensity looking at us ... were meant as an appeal or as a menace. What were we who had strayed in here? Could we handle that dumb thing, or would it handle us? I felt how big, how confoundedly big, was that thing that couldn't talk, and perhaps was deaf as well. What was in there? I could see a little ivory coming out from there, and I had heard Mr. Kurtz was in there. (81)

The source of plunder coming out of its depths, Kurtz is ambiguously associated with the jungle into which Marlow must sail. In preparation, his steamboat must be recovered and repaired, a task that The Manager estimates should take three months to complete. Marlow's dedication to his task provides him with a sense of purpose amid the general ennui: he sets to work the day after arriving at the Central Station. Living aboard his command distances him even further from the pilgrims as it asserts his dedication to the Victorian 'work ethic'. Set against this is the incompetence of the system: the rivets Marlow requires lie in the dirt at the Coastal Station where, burst from their cases, they had even 'rolled into the grove of death' (83). In the view of Cedric Watts, this apparent incompetence is a ruse engineered by The Manager, behind which lies a high order of competence, for it intentionally delays 'the relief' of Kurtz (1984: 119–21).

Like his Roman counterpart nearly two centuries earlier, on whom Britain exerted 'the fascination of the abomination' (50), Marlow is both attracted to and alienated by the surrounding jungle. This ambivalence is consistent with his predicament generally: character and narrator, he is both in the tale and out of it; one of the European 'invaders' of Africa, yet increasingly set apart by his scepticism and sympathies. Amid the rumour mill at work among the pilgrims, Marlow discovers himself associated with Kurtz, 'of the new gang – the gang of virtue', thanks to his aunt's 'influential acquaintances' (79), an illusion he fosters in order to add urgency to his demand for rivets. In the event, this has little bearing, but the ruse occasions Marlow's judgement on lies: 'You know I hate, detest, and can't bear a lie ... it appals me. There is a taint of death, a flavour of mortality in lies – which is exactly what I hate and detest in the world – what I want to forget' (82). Marlow's claim seems to impinge directly on the 'civilizing mission' whose 'philanthropic pretence' he has already observed first-hand. But he also confesses that, in maintaining the pretence of his standing in the Company, he 'went near enough' to lying, reminding us that Marlow too is part of this 'mission'. A Company employee, his values are necessarily tainted by association: 'I became in an instant as much of a pretence as the rest of the pilgrims' (82). His may be an isolated critical voice, but it would lose some of its testamentary force were he not personally implicated. Marlow is in some guise like Coleridge's Ancient Mariner, driven to tell of things that he wants to forget.

Explaining that he believed then that his pretence 'would be of help to that Kurtz', Marlow interrupts his narrative at this point to appeal to his audience: 'Do you see him? Do you see the story? Do you see anything?' As if replicating the impossibility of conveying and the difficulty of confessing his experience, Marlow's story breaks off at this point: 'He was silent for a while' (82). The interruption has an obvious dramatic impact, suggesting the overwhelming impression made on him by Kurtz, but it also facilitates the critical distance that allows for Marlow's interpretive overview of his task, a narrating consciousness self-consciously commenting upon its own progress, and with it the suspicion that the further he travels into the African interior, the deeper he journeys into the depths of his own psyche: 'it is impossible to convey the life-sensation of any given epoch of one's existence – that which makes its truth, its meaning – its subtle and penetrating essence. It is impossible. We live, as we dream – alone . . . .' (82). It is at this point, by which time Marlow has become 'no more to us than a voice', that the frame-narrator voices his impressions about the 'faint uneasiness' inspired by the tale. Atmospherically, the conditions in which the tale is heard on the Thames – 'pitch dark'; 'the heavy night-air on the river' – replicate those within the tale itself, reminding us of the claim that the meaning of Marlow's stories 'was not inside like a kernel but outside, enveloping the tale which brought it out' (48). Furthermore, as impressions of colonized Africa are palimpsestically overlaid on those of the Thames, the two 'worlds' are drawn into an inescapable relationship.

Instead of the rivets Marlow requires, 'there came an invasion, an infliction, a visitation' (87): the Eldorado Exploring Expedition, headed by The Manager's uncle. Described as 'sordid buccaneers' who 'infested' the station, they conform to amoral, rapacious type: 'To tear treasure out of the bowels of the land was their desire, with no more moral purpose at the back of it than there is in burglars breaking into a safe' (87). By way of contrast, and setting up the opposition between Kurtz and the other Europeans that will direct his narrative, the first part of *Heart of Darkness*, concludes with Marlow's wondering whether Kurtz, 'who had come out equipped with moral ideas of some sort, would climb to the top after all and how he would set about his work when there' (88).

PART II: FROM THE CENTRAL STATION TO THE INNER STATION

Part II opens with Marlow's inadvertent eavesdropping on a conversation between The Manager and his uncle, that, as he belatedly recognizes, concerns Kurtz, and in which it transpires that Kurtz 'asked the Administration to be sent' into the Interior 'with the idea of showing what he could do' (89). Presenting such information obliquely, before we know that it refers to Kurtz, constitutes a further example of delayed decoding, and interpreting the tantalizingly incomplete information necessarily means that the reader shares Marlow's predicament. The Manager's attitude towards Kurtz is evident: he bemoans Kurtz's influence, and takes refuge in the fact that the climate may 'do away with this difficulty' (89). Part of the scramble for loot is the competing self-interests of the Europeans themselves: they not only steal from the Africans but are ready to intrigue and even 'kill' each other – at least by delaying action. Marlow later admits to succumbing to 'the playful paw-strokes of the wilderness' (105) during the upriver journey. Kurtz's last communication from the Inner Station was received over a year ago, when he sent back the assistant who had been assigned to him, but, to The Manager's chagrin, he continues to send ivory, 'lots of it – prime sort – lots – most annoying, from him' (90). It transpires that, having accompanied the ivory some three hundred miles downriver, Kurtz apparently decided not to return to the Central Station and left the task to his English half-caste clerk. Instead, he returned to the interior, providing the listening Marlow with his first 'distinct glimpse' of the man: 'the dugout, four paddling savages, and the lone white man turning his back suddenly on the headquarters, on relief, on thoughts of home – perhaps; setting his face towards the depths of the wilderness' (90). This image of heroic intrepidity gains as the conversation continues.

When The Manager bemoans the presence of a European competitor for ivory, his uncle's response suggests the prevailing state of moral dereliction: 'get him hanged! Why not? Anything – anything can be done in this country', adding: 'The danger is in Europe.' In sharp contrast, Kurtz's belief, quoted by The Manager, offers a philanthropic alternative, blending trade and morality: 'Each station should be like a beacon on the road towards better things, a centre for trade of course, but also for humanizing, improving, instructing' (91). It is, therefore, unsurprising that Marlow should throw his lot in with Kurtz even before meeting him. The uncle's advice to his nephew, who fears that Kurtz will replace him as station manager, is to trust to the fact that, unlike the other Europeans, his health remains unaffected by the climate. Then, in a gesture that combines elements of the grotesque and the audacious, the uncle extends 'his short flipper of an arm', seeming to beckon in 'a treacherous appeal to the lurking death, to the hidden evil, to the profound darkness' (92) of the land. So startled is Marlow that he betrays his presence aboard the steamboat and the pair return to the station, their departure providing an image of the 'patient' wilderness's resistance to the 'fantastic invasion', as their shadows trail 'over the tall grass without bending a single blade'. With meaningful juxtaposition, shortly afterwards the Eldorado Expedition enters the wilderness 'that closed upon it as the sea closes over a diver', its fate unrecorded beyond Marlow's speculation: 'They, no doubt, like the rest of us, found what they deserved' (92).

At this point the narrative advances in the form of a summary: 'It was just two months from the day we left the creek when we came to the bank below Kurtz's station' (92). From this vantage, Marlow's account of the actual voyage, that occupies the rest of Part II, is retrospective. Such temporal dislocation only adds to the sense of cultural, moral and psychological lost bearings. The narrative's chronological instability also helps to convey the impression that Marlow is attempting to craft recollected and rearranged impressions into a coherent form.

From the outset, Marlow's literal river journey assumes metaphorical and metaphysical implications, a journey into the unresolvable, as the narrative seems to be searching for a language to match the audacity of the truths it attempts to communicate about the nature of man. It begins with his observation that 'Going up that river was like travelling back to the earliest beginnings of the world' (92), adding to the suggestive mythic parallels that surround the journey upriver humankind's return to a lost Eden – and with it another Fall. As the steamboat crawls, in Marlow's imagination at least, 'towards Kurtz – exclusively' (95), the setting is redefined as primeval and threatening, an alienating expanse in which he feels progressively cut off from his roots: memories of his past return 'in the shape of an unrestful and noisy dream, remembered with wonder amongst the overwhelming realities of this strange world of plants, and water, and silence' (93), while the 'earth seemed unearthly' (96). Marlow feels himself to have entered an unknown world, and as the steamboat carries him deeper into Africa, so his sense of estrangement from the world he knows increases.

The sheer scale of the jungle dwarfs the steamboat, repeatedly likened to a beetle, and, while disorienting Marlow, the factual presence of the wilderness is transformed through mythopoeic substitution into a watchful, embodied stillness, 'the stillness of an implacable force brooding over an inscrutable intention' (93). The overwhelming impression of the environment on him – 'Trees, trees, millions of trees, massive, running up high' (95) – recalls the opening lines of Dante's *Inferno*: 'Half way along the road we have to go, / I found myself obscured in a great forest, / Bewildered, and I knew I had lost my way' (Canto 1).

Initially a symbol of alienation and energy, as Marlow's journey progresses the jungle is reconstituted as an expression of forces that cannot be contained or controlled. As he did at the Central Station, Marlow is distracted and sustained by work, which provides a bulwark of reality against the dreamlike and hypnotic sensations conjured up by the journey. Travelling at a rate of eight miles every three hours, on an upriver journey lasting two months, Marlow is exercised by the task of keeping his steamboat powered with supplies of wood, repairing its pipes and boiler, and, above all, navigating his course through unfamiliar waters, his professionalism marked by confessions of how he felt every time he scraped the riverbed. As he says, 'When you have to attend to things of that sort, to the mere incidents of the surface, the reality – the reality, I tell you – fades. The inner truth is hidden – luckily, luckily' (93).

In this, and casting a further slur upon the indolence of the pilgrims, Marlow is assisted by Africans – and not merely Africans but cannibals to boot. Enlisted along the way, these 'Fine fellows . . . were men one could work with' (94). Overtly, the cannibal crew ensure that the estrangement wrought on Marlow by his African experience extends to the realm of moral estrangement, through social taboo. But their capacity for work also complicates any sense of social superiority he might be expected to feel, since, like him, the cannibals embody the Victorian principle of the work ethic, given moral, religious and philosophical resonances in the writings of Thomas Carlyle. Marlow's literal navigation of the river carrying him 'deeper and deeper into the heart of darkness' (95) is simultaneously figured as a navigation into human values and potential, his uncertain perceptions reflecting those of the reader negotiating the twists and turns of the text.

Their supply of rotten hippo-meat thrown overboard by the 'pilgrims', the crew are left with 'a few lumps of some stuff like half-cooked dough, of a dirty lavender colour' (104). According to Albert J. Guerard, 'Conrad here operates through ambiguous suggestion (are the lumps human flesh?)' (1958: 35). The fact that Marlow goes on to comment that the crew 'now and then swallowed a piece ... but so small that it seemed done more for the looks of the thing than for any serious purpose of sustenance' (104) suggests that the food serves a ritual rather than practical purpose and, in terms of social rites, the debasement of the religious rationale for the colonial venture (expressed through the platitudes of Marlow's aunt and the pilgrims themselves) extends naturally to the parody of the Eucharist in the references to cannibalism. None the less, as the literary examples of Juvenal, Montaigne and others have demonstrated, the imputation of cannibalism is often fuelled by an ethnic agenda: what *they* do is inadmissible among *us*. The very etymology of the word 'cannibal', coined by Christopher Columbus from the name of the Carib natives of the Caribbean, reveals its racialist origins.

The designation of the Africans as an undifferentiated mass is often reductive: the crew are 'cannibals'; their counterparts ashore, 'prehistoric man', are glimpsed as 'a burst of yells, a whirl of black limbs, a mass of hands clapping, of feet stamping, of bodies swaying, of eyes rolling' (96). Most jarringly, Marlow's narrative is casually racist in its recourse to terms like 'savage' and 'nigger', reminding the reader that such was the currency of his colonial age and, unsurprisingly, in our time charges of racism have been levelled against the novella as well as Conrad himself. Caution must be exercised here for, to charge as 'racist' a text whose terms were common parlance is wilfully to overlook both the claims of historical context and the notion of social progress that expects the present to have learned from the past. That Conrad was aware of the offence given by such terminology is evident in his earlier novel, *The Nigger of the 'Narcissus'* (1897), where James Wait reacts angrily to Belfast, with racial abuse of his own: 'You wouldn't call me nigger if I wasn't half dead, you Irish beggar!' (79–80). When *The Nigger of the 'Narcissus'* was first published in the United States it was re-christened *The Children of the Sea*. Risibly, however, publishers insisted on the change on purely racist grounds: 'The argument was that the American public would not read a book about a "nigger"' (Smith n.d.: 8).

Given his international experience as a merchant seaman, Marlow seems surprisingly naive in his expectations about Africa, where, shocked out of his innocence/ignorance, he passes the judgements that transcend his age. But, to say this is to run the risk of wanting it both ways: *Heart of Darkness* is and isn't a racist text – inevitably so in its historicized reality, it yet counters the attitudes of its time. So how does this work in practice? One of the Africans aboard the steamboat takes on the job of fireman. This is how Marlow describes him:

> And between whiles I had to look after the savage who was fireman. He was an improved specimen; he could fire up a vertical boiler. He was there below me, and, upon my word, to look at him was as edifying as seeing a dog in a parody of breeches and a feather hat, walking on his hind-legs. A few months of training had done for that really fine chap. He squinted at the steam-gauge and at the water-gauge with an evident effort of intrepidity – and he had filed teeth, too, the poor devil, and the wool of his pate shaved into queer patterns, and three ornamental scars on each of his cheeks. He ought to have been clapping his hands and stamping his feet on the bank, instead of which he was hard at work, a thrall to strange witchcraft, full of improving knowledge. He was useful because he had been instructed; and what he knew was this – that should the water in that transparent thing disappear, the evil spirit inside the boiler would get angry through the greatness of its thirst, and take a terrible vengeance. So he sweated and fired up and watched the glass fearfully (with an impromptu charm, made of rags, tied to his arm, and a piece

> of polished bone, as big as a watch, stuck flatways through his lower lip), while the wooded banks slipped past us slowly, the short noise was left behind, the interminable miles of silence – and we crept on, towards Kurtz. (97–8)

There is, surely, enough here to support a contemporary charge of racism. First, the terminology is racist: the African is referred to a 'savage' (with the implication that Europeans are 'civilized'); secondly, the language of European mechanization and science (whereby the fireman is a 'specimen') is set against African 'witchcraft' and 'superstition'; and, thirdly, the portrait of the African, emphasizing his exotic appearance, is clearly designed to render him as the 'Other' to Western readers. So far, so racist.

But another latent and contrasting reading subverts this. First, that claim about the fireman looking like 'a dog in breeches with a feather hat' echoes Dr Samuel Johnson's comment about women preachers, reminding us how cultural and gendered 'Othering' resorts to comparably crude codes of diminution: 'A woman's preaching is like a dog's walking on his hinder legs. It is not done well; but you are surprised to find it done at all' (Boswell 1791; 1924: 285). So, Marlow's comment draws upon the language of Western reason, to which the 'good sense' of Dr Johnson contributed in no small measure, with all of its obvious flaws. Secondly, however alien to the fireman is the technology required to run a steamboat, and however much it translates into his language of witchcraft and superstition, he does, none the less, accomplish the task. And, finally, the tone of Marlow's comments here clearly suggests that his sympathy is with the fireman: when he says that 'A few months of training had done for that really fine chap', he is saying that the African has been ruined by his contact with Europeans.

Look especially at the sentence: 'He ought to have been clapping his hands and stamping his feet on the bank, instead of which he was hard at work, a thrall to strange witchcraft, full of improving knowledge.' Here Marlow uses the language of morality ('ought') to suggest that the fireman has been reduced, not elevated, by his contact with Europeans, and the phrase 'improving knowledge' is clearly ironic. We might note, too, that when 'witchcraft' is employed here, it describes European technology. In this manner, Marlow turns the tables upon the Europeans by presenting the African's perspective: to the fireman it is *we* who engage in witchcraft. In short, Marlow is racist – and needs to be if he is to reflect the colonialist attitudes of his age – and, at the same time, Marlow is not racist, because his racial sympathies lie with the African rather than the European. This double authority, whereby *Heart of Darkness* both reflects and transcends its historical moment, contributes to its enduring appeal.

Within the narrative, too, Marlow's experience is audaciously located outside known time and space. His surroundings are configured in atavistic terms – Africa is 'prehistoric earth ... an unknown planet' (95) – while the reactions of the natives to the presence of the steamboat remain unfathomable: 'The prehistoric man was cursing us, praying to us, welcoming us – who could tell?' (96). But while this fuels such sentiments as: 'We were cut off from the comprehension of our surroundings' and the suspicion that 'we were travelling in the night of first ages' (96), it might also be seen to reduce the natives to an earlier stage of human evolution. Again, however, this judgement needs qualification. For, not only do they embody the quintessence of humanity, 'truth stripped of its cloak of time' (97), but, as the example of the hungry cannibals aboard the steamboat demonstrates, the very quality of restraint they manifest is precisely what is lacking in their 'civilized' European counterparts. For all that his language and attitudes are European, Marlow judges men on the basis of individual worth rather than race or culture.

The atavistic sense that Marlow has of the Africans as 'prehistoric' initially seems disparaging and designed to confirm nineteenth-century racial theories about evolution that, at their crudest, lent support to the belief that certain races are destined to subjugation by others. However, this belief is overturned through a 'thrilling' identification:

> They howled and leaped, and spun, and made horrid faces; but what thrilled you was just the thought of their humanity – like yours – the thought of your remote kinship with this wild

> and passionate uproar. Ugly. Yes, it was ugly enough; but if you were man enough you would admit to yourself that there was in you just the faintest trace of a response to the terrible frankness of that noise, a dim suspicion of there being a meaning in it which you – you so remote from the night of first ages – could comprehend. (96)

The sense of kinship with what he sees as a residual, constituent part of his make-up as a human being is troubling to Marlow because of the threat this identification poses for his civilized self-definition. None the less, when one of his listeners aboard the *Nellie* reacts to this provocative identification, Marlow's response is majestic: 'for good or evil mine is the speech that cannot be silenced' (97).

Fifty miles below the Inner Station the party come across a deserted reed-hut where, upon the welcome supply of firewood left for them, is a note advising them to 'Approach cautiously' (98). Among the debris, Marlow discovers a book, *An Inquiry into some Points of Seamanship*, 'by a man Tower, Towson – some such name – Master in His Majesty's Navy'. The timing of the find is apposite: with Kurtz's station just over two days' sail away, the book, which reflects 'an honest concern for the right way of going to work', represents a final reminder of a code of values to which Marlow can subscribe before he reaches his destination. He calls it 'something unmistakably real' (99), while concluding, mistakenly as it turns out, that the notes pencilled in the margins are written in cipher. They are in fact in Russian.

Two days afterwards, now only some eight miles from Kurtz's station, the fading daylight and the hazardous navigation make further progress dangerous, and Marlow casts anchor for the night. The silent jungle seems 'changed into stone', inducing one 'to suspect yourself of being deaf – and the night came suddenly, and struck you blind as well' (101). While these are only impressions, the sensory deprivation, as if bearing out Marlow's observation that the 'essentials of this affair lay deep under the surface' (100), suggestively redefines his quest as a psychological rather than a physical journey, with the implication that the wilderness into which Marlow is travelling serves as a symbol of the unconscious. This suggestion gains when the next morning brings a white fog, 'more blinding than the night' (101), blurring the outlines of the steamer 'as though she had been on the point of dissolving' (102), and Marlow's impression of 'the dream-sensation that pervaded all my days at that time' (105). In this manner, exotic adventure narrative is refashioned as psychological adventure narrative, and Marlow's tale about the historical exploitation of Africa is simultaneously an exploration and exposure of the latent human capacity behind such exploitation.

Emanating from the fog, the company hear 'a cry, a very loud cry, as of infinite desolation' that culminates in 'intolerably excessive shrieking' (101–2). While the sounds compound the suspenseful warning about proceeding with caution, they equally reinforce the suggestion that the setting is alive: to Marlow it seems as though 'the mist itself had screamed' (102). The outburst anticipates the attack on the steamboat that, when it comes, Marlow recognizes as 'really an attempt at repulse': 'it was undertaken under the stress of desperation, and in its essence was purely protective' (107). As the pilgrims hurriedly arm themselves with rifles, the hungry cannibals begin to anticipate a feast – 'Catch 'im ... Eat 'im' (103) – prompting Marlow's speculation upon their restraint in not attacking the company aboard the steamboat, whom they greatly outnumber. The placement of this observation is strategic, harking back to the excesses of the pilgrims that Marlow has witnessed thus far and serving as a reminder of self-control before the encounter with Kurtz, who, it transpires later, ordered the attack (139). To Marlow the cries from the natives hidden in the jungle along the riverbank carry 'an irresistible impression of sorrow' and 'a great human passion let loose' (107). Thus, the 'attack' is partly palliated even before it happens, both by the ambiguity that inspires it (why should aggression be an expression of 'sorrow'?), and by Marlow's suggestion that the cry that precedes it affirms something definitively human.

When the expected attack occurs, it is initially misinterpreted. Restricted to Marlow's perspective, the event is presented in a series of delayed decodings within which the belated recognition that the 'Sticks, little sticks' flying about are, in fact, 'Arrows, by Jove!' (109, 110) is emblematic of a broader misreading of the situation, that includes his puzzlement as to why the pole-man suddenly lies down on the deck or the fireman sits down abruptly before his furnace. As elsewhere, Marlow's subjective vision is recreated in his narration, ensuring its re-enactment in the reader's interpretive process. Orientation problems are bathetically extended to navigating as Marlow's vision of a snag in the river is obscured by the smoke discharged from the pilgrims' rifles, fired wildly into the jungle. The episode is marked by a further, and tragic, lack of restraint involving the helmsman's death. The 'fool-nigger' (111) throws open the shutter of the pilot-house to join in the shooting, and, continuing to brandish his empty rifle, is felled by a spear. In Marlow's judgement, 'He had no restraint, no restraint – just like Kurtz' (119). Graphically illustrating Marlow's encounter with the literal horrors of the country, the helmsman falls back, hitting his head against the wheel, where Marlow has replaced him, before falling dead at his feet. As the helmsman's blood fills his shoes, Marlow sounds the ship's steam-whistle, successfully scaring away the attackers, whose 'tumult of angry and warlike yells' is replaced by 'such a tremulous and prolonged wail of mournful fear and utter despair as may be imagined to follow the flight of the last hope from the earth' (112).

Not unnaturally, Marlow's interpretation of events is: 'I suppose that Mr. Kurtz is dead as well by this time', with the implication that his journey has been in vain; but he goes further, confessing his realization, even as he is busy throwing his bloody shoes and socks into the river, that 'exactly' what he had been looking forward to en route was 'a talk with Kurtz', who 'presented himself as a voice' (113). Comparing the resulting 'extravagance of emotion' he feels to the 'howling sorrow' from the jungle, he describes his sensation of loss as analogous to being 'robbed of a belief' or missing his 'destiny' (114), which one of his listeners characterizes as 'absurd', while the juxtaposition of the natives' despair and these comments about Kurtz unites the two in the reader's mind, enabling us to predict a connection between them.

At this point Marlow appears to lose control of his story, creating the impression that his invocation of Kurtz overwhelms the telling. First, a short pause ensues as he relights his pipe, and when he resumes it is not to tell the story but to counteract the charge that his sentiments were 'absurd': pointing to the 'normal' lives of his audience, he declares that they lack the breadth of experience to judge his experiences. Instead of returning to the story of the attack, he gives away some of the plot in advance by announcing that he did have the 'privilege' of hearing Kurtz, 'very little more than a voice', and then, from the perspective of hindsight, he admits that the 'impalpable' memory of this time is composed of a medley of 'voices' that linger 'like a dying vibration'. Included in the chronological instability is the claim: 'I laid the ghost of his gifts at last with a lie' (115), which, although the reader cannot know it at this point, is a summary of the story's final act. Also having a bearing on the ending is the brief, but quickly dismissed, reference to 'the girl' together with the claim that 'the women ... should be out of it. We must help them to stay in that beautiful world of their own, lest ours gets worse' (115). But, in sequence, such comments contribute to the reader's sense of disorientation, further unsettling the narrative as Kurtz's presence becomes more overt. The retrospective comments on Kurtz that follow locate Marlow outside the tale he is telling, looking back with the benefit of complete knowledge while, simultaneously, influencing the reader's future reception of Kurtz.

Fittingly at the centre of this haunted narrative, Kurtz is described in cadaverous terms, a 'disinterred body', whose head, 'patted' by the wilderness, resembles 'an ivory ball'. He has been transformed into the object of his obsession. Within the tale's symbolic register, the wilderness, finding itself invaded by him, invades Kurtz in turn. In terms that range from the tender and sensuous to the vampiric and diabolic, Marlow explains how the wilderness overwhelmed this European Renaissance man: 'it had taken him, loved him, embraced him, got into his veins, consumed his flesh, and sealed his soul to its own by the inconceivable ceremonies of some devilish initiation' (115). The African wilderness is now less a geographical place than a symbolic space that reflects and accommodates European dreams of wealth and power. If this transforms Africa into a function of European fantasy, then it also reveals how Africa reduces and transcends such fantasies. Even the scope of Kurtz's overweening megalomania is belittled: ' "My Intended, my ivory, my station, my river, my –" everything belonged to him. It made me hold my breath in expectation of hearing the wilderness burst into a prodigious peal of laughter that would shake the fixed stars in their places' (116). As Marlow, who is haunted by the call to which Kurtz succumbs, says, it is less a case of what belonged to Kurtz than 'to know what he belonged to, how many powers of darkness claimed him for their own' (116).

It quickly becomes apparent why Kurtz is the best agent of the Company, which equates to gathering the most ivory: because of his unrestrained rapacity and brutality. Emphatically denying that he is trying 'to excuse or even explain' (117) Kurtz's actions, Marlow none the less places them within an understandable but deeply unsettling context:

> He had taken his seat amongst the devils of the land – I mean literally. You can't understand. How could you? – with solid pavement under your feet, surrounded by kind neighbours ready to cheer you or to fall on you, stepping delicately between the butcher and the policeman, in the holy terror of scandal and gallows and lunatic asylums – how could you imagine what particular region of the first ages a man's untrammelled feet may take him into by way of solitude – utter solitude without a policeman – by way of silence – utter silence, where no warning voice of a kind neighbour can be heard whispering of public opinion? These little things make all the great difference. (116)

The implications of this for any civilized self-definition are profound. Morality is relative not absolute. Far from being innate, our moral behaviour is consequential upon the strictures of the situations we find ourselves in. At its most extreme, this suggests that we all have the capacity to behave like Kurtz, and the reason that we do not is because we lack the opportunity. Instead, it is fear of the social consequences of our actions that determines behaviour. From this angle, marooned in this wild country where previous rules don't apply and social censure is absent, Kurtz acts out latent desires that the rest of us repress. However exorbitant seem Marlow's claims, it is the fact that they are applied to Kurtz that gives us pause. When Marlow says, 'All Europe contributed to the making of Kurtz' (117), more than his parentage – his mother half-English; his father half-French – is implied. A 'universal genius', painter, writer, 'essentially a great musician', who 'would have been a splendid leader of an extreme party' (154), Kurtz is a protean figure, the apogee of civilized man, and yet even he has fallen. The tacit question this invites is: if *he* can go wrong, what chance for the rest of us?

The report that Kurtz prepares for the International Society for the Suppression of Savage Customs provides an illustration of the effect of his sojourn in Africa, charting his slide into moral dereliction. Beginning with such high-minded sentiments as 'By the simple exercise of our will we can exert a power for good practically unbounded', it concludes with the 'scrawled' postscript: 'Exterminate all the brutes!' (118). Venturing to Africa with civilizing intent, Kurtz ended up presiding 'at certain midnight dances ending with unspeakable rites, which ... were offered up to him' (118). That these rites should be 'unspeakable' is part of the poetics of *Heart of Darkness*: the narrative suggests rather than enforces meaning in order to implicate the reader in the atmosphere surrounding the story. In this case, Marlow relies upon his audience to fill in the gap with their individual nightmare-visions, while generating what we might call a 'rhetoric of the unsayable' to suggest that Kurtz's actions cannot be spoken.

The discussion of Kurtz concludes with a return to the narrative present, through Marlow's comment that, while Kurtz left an indelible mark on him, he is 'not prepared to affirm the fellow was exactly worth the life we lost in getting to him. I missed my late helmsman awfully' (119). Yet, while praising the helmsman's contribution of honest labour – 'he had done something, he had steered' – Marlow traces his demise to a comparable flaw: 'He had no restraint, no restraint – just like Kurtz' (119). Increasingly, this capacity for restraint is presented as a safeguard against threats to morality and, as here, life itself. Having tipped the helmsman's body into the river, to be eaten by fishes rather than the cannibals, Marlow takes charge of the wheel and, soon afterwards, the steamboat finally arrives at her destination, the Inner Station.

It is while scanning the station through binoculars from the safe vantage of the ship that Marlow sees the 'round carved balls' ornamenting the posts near the house and which, in a further and shocking instance of delayed decoding, are subsequently identified as human skulls. Grisly as these images are, their most shocking aspect, as scholarship has demonstrated, is that Conrad's fictional account of the European invasion of Africa drew upon literal fact. For instance, the Congo diary of the Swedish missionary E. J. Glave, which was published in *The Century Magazine* in September 1897, records how the *Force publique* officer, Léon Rom, ornamented the flower bed in front of his house with twenty-one human skulls. (The claims were repeated in the *Saturday Review* of 17 December 1898.)

Marlow is guided into shore by a white man whose patched clothes give him the appearance of a harlequin, a figure from the *commedia dell'arte* tradition, dressed in multi-coloured clothing, who approximates the trickster. Appropriately his facial expressions suggest that his clothes replicate his personality: 'His face was like the autumn sky, overcast one moment and bright the next' (122). 'You English?' asks Marlow, seeking a mirroring nationality, and is disappointed to find that the man isn't. (Marlow speaks English with both The Harlequin and Kurtz.) Instead he turns out to be Russian, and a fellow sailor, who had been 'wandering about that river for nearly two years alone' (124). Confirming the international presence in the country, the 'harlequin' also contributes to the sense of European identity as destabilized there. He, too, confirms the spell cast by Kurtz's words, claiming: 'You don't talk with that man – you listen to him' and 'this man has enlarged my mind' (123, 125). This section of the narrative concludes by confirming Marlow's suspicions about the attack on the steamboat, and reaffirming Kurtz's ambiguous status as tyrant-deity, as The Harlequin says of the natives: 'They don't want him to go' (124–5).

PART III: THE CENTRAL STATION, KURTZ, AND MARLOW'S RETURN TO EUROPE

The third and final part of the novella begins where Part II left off, continuing Marlow's conversation with the young Russian sailor. Part of Marlow's experience of Africa, The Harlequin is viewed as 'fabulous', 'inexplicable', 'bewildering', and 'an insoluble problem' (126). Indeed, so extraordinary seems this youth that, after their parting, Marlow wonders 'whether I had ever really seen him – whether it was possible to meet such a phenomenon!' (140). In The Harlequin's own words, and reminding the reader that Kurtz's absorption by his surroundings is shared by other Europeans, including Marlow, his presence in the wilderness has involved venturing 'a little farther ... then still a little farther – till I had gone so far that I don't know how I'll ever get back' (126). Despite his appearance, 'in motley', the traditional garb of the Fool, The Harlequin's place in the story is crucial, not least because, as his patchwork clothes suggest, he too reflects the fragmentation of European identity that provides one of the tale's central themes – and can be seen, in post-colonial terms, as resistance to the colonial invasion. As if to confirm this, The Harlequin is presented ambiguously: for instance, he is protected from the wilderness by his innocence, while his words about Kurtz are spoken 'with mingled eagerness and reluctance' (128). The Harlequin also exists as a precursor, in the way that, say, John the Baptist does for Christ – not as an explicit allusion to this, but in the tradition of the precursor figure.

The Russian's experiences in addition provide a further frame of expectation for Marlow's imminent meeting with Kurtz. This apologist for Kurtz, who he feels has been 'shamefully abandoned' (132) by his fellow Europeans, has served in the capacities of confidant, nurse, pander, and whipping-boy. Left with an unshakable 'devotion' to Kurtz, which Marlow considers 'about the most dangerous thing in every way he had come upon so far' (127), his account provides in brief outline the details of Kurtz's decline into barbarity, from his early ivory expeditions that included discovering a lake, to running out of trade goods and resorting to raiding the country, with the help of a tribe to whom he had come 'with thunder and lightning' and who accord him the status of a deity. On one occasion he threatened to shoot The Harlequin for a little ivory in his possession, simply 'because he could do so, and had a fancy for it, and there was nothing on earth to prevent him killing whom he jolly well pleased' (128). To Marlow, Kurtz is simply 'mad' (129). But to The Harlequin, 'Kurtz's last disciple' (132) and enthralled by his eloquence, 'You can't judge Mr. Kurtz as you would an ordinary man' (128). Conrad's fictions repeatedly return to the subject of man at the end of his tether, placed in a situation that will test his endurance to breaking point and in which he is forced back upon his inner strength. Kurtz, who 'lacked restraint in the gratification of his various lusts' (131), provides an extreme example of this: 'But the wilderness had found him out early, and had taken on him a terrible vengeance for the fantastic invasion. I think it had whispered to him things about himself which he did not know, things of which he had no conception till he took counsel with this great solitude – and the whisper had proved irresistibly fascinating. It echoed loudly within him because he was hollow at the core. . . .' (131).

Detached from European society and its strictures, Kurtz has entered a realm in which the excesses of his imagination and desires can wander freely. Lacking any moral system to curb his actions, Kurtz's megalomania has led him to demand unlimited, deific powers. The physically debilitating effects of the jungle upon him act as a metaphor for the morally debilitating effects of his unchecked desires, casting the wilderness as a representation of man's hidden, unconscious potential.

It is during his conversation with the Russian that Marlow experiences the shocking revelation that the 'ornamental' balls around Kurtz's hut are, in fact, human heads. The moment provides a mini-triumph of narrative technique, accentuating perspective at a moment when contrasted visions of Kurtz are juxtaposed: Marlow's use of binoculars serves to bring these grisly emblems of Kurtz's depravity 'within reach of my hand', only to have them leap as quickly into 'inaccessible distance' (130, 131) when he puts the glasses down again. Propelling the objects of Marlow's gaze into nearer and further relief stylistically recreates, in a single image, the interpretive problem confronting both Marlow and his audience: how is Kurtz to be judged, in terms of predetermined mores; or is he in some way beyond these, 'inaccessible', because he has entered a field for which there are no foreknown limits? On the surface, Kurtz's actions damn him, unambiguously. But if they are manifestations of latent human potential evoked irresistibly by and mirrored in the wilderness, that is simultaneously external space and interior state, could they, however perversely, designate him as victim rather than criminal?

The Harlequin's claim that these human heads belonged to 'rebels' further compounds the issue of perspective, albeit within the admittedly narrow sphere of a Eurocentric vision that subjects the Africans to repeated redefinition: 'Rebels! What would be the next definition I was to hear? There had been enemies, criminals, workers – and these were rebels' (132). But Marlow silences him when he begins explaining how native chiefs would crawl before Kurtz, believing that the 'uncomplicated savagery' evidenced in the tangible heads is preferable to the imagined ceremonies of abasement that transport him 'into some lightless region of subtle horrors' (132). Again, the issue of perspective obtrudes: Marlow is happier – to use the word loosely – dealing with what is tangible than with what is intangible. This attitude does pose a problem, since the narrative insists upon a reading that blurs actual and psychological events, transforming manifest realities into expressions of latent compulsion. In a sense it cannot be otherwise: first, because the tale of Kurtz is of someone who acts out his desires; and, second, because it is predicated on the fact that his desires are, potentially at least, similar to anyone else's, but his circumstances enable him to transmute them into action.

A further point to note here concerns the apparent willingness of the natives and The Harlequin to worship Kurtz and turn him into a fetish. Why they do so and how this sham operates is never fully explained, beyond the fear that his brutality instils. Is Kurtz, for instance, intended as a parallel sham to the *mission civilisatrice*? Furthermore, as the religious imagery surrounding Kurtz demonstrates, through him Conrad is dismantling aspects of the human psyche in general, not just those of the Europeans.

Kurtz finally makes his appearance in the narrative, being carried towards the steamboat on an improvised stretcher towards the steamboat. The rescue party, which also bears his armaments – four guns, derided by the watching Marlow as 'the thunderbolts of that pitiful Jupiter' (134) – is checked in its process by a cry of lamentation 'whose shrillness pierced the still air like an arrow flying straight to the very heart of the land' (133). The simile draws its force from the immediate appearance of hitherto concealed natives, armed with spears and bows, who do not want to see Kurtz go, as well as from the contrast it points up between the types of weaponry. It is the skeletal 'atrocious phantom' (133), Kurtz himself, who orders their withdrawal. The contrast between his authoritative infirmity and their subordinated vitality is viewed through Marlow's binoculars: 'It was as though an animated image of death carved out of old ivory had been shaking its hand with menaces at a motionless crowd of men made of dark and glittering bronze' (134). Fittingly, to add to the contradictions that compose Kurtz – including Marlow's wry observation that, despite his name meaning 'short' in German, he looks over seven feet tall – having waited so long to hear Kurtz talk, the distance between them means that this sequence in presented in dumbshow, in which it appears that, true to his reputation, Kurtz seems to want to 'swallow all the air, all the earth, all the men before him' (134). The invalid appearance of Kurtz seems designed to unsettle his 'extraordinary' reputation. That this leading light of the Company, invested with godlike status by his followers, should turn out to be such a 'pitiful Jupiter' provides not only a corrective to the self-proclaimed superiority of the colonial European but also, and drawing upon this, a more general subversion of the image of the Nietzschean Superman or *Übermensch* that would bedevil European politics in the century after the novella's publication. That said, Kurtz is, of course, not typical of European colonialism. Rather, he is its extreme manifestation.

Aboard the steamer, Kurtz is housed in one of the cabins, where the correspondence awaiting him includes a letter containing a 'special recommendation' relating to Marlow, to whom his first words are: 'I am glad.' Marlow's excited reaction is tempered by ambiguity: 'A voice! a voice! It was grave, profound, vibrating, while the man did not seem capable of a whisper' (135). While recalling Marlow's earlier judgement that Kurtz was 'very little more than a voice' (115) – and, in turn, the frame-narrator's designation of Marlow as 'no more to us than a voice' (83) – the incongruity between the voice and the speaker, between appearance and reality, sustains the impression that he is, in some sense, indefinable.

The appearance of Kurtz's African mistress, 'a wild and gorgeous apparition of a woman' (135), identifies the exotic setting as an erotic space, a fairly standard trope in colonial adventure writings and, contradictorily, in making the Other an object of desire, a connection that undermines the us/them distinction upon which colonialism is founded. The paragraph-long description of the woman that follows is worth quoting in its entirety:

> She walked with measured steps, draped in striped and fringed cloths, treading the earth proudly, with a slight jingle and flash of barbarous ornaments. She carried her head high; her hair was done in the shape of a helmet; she had brass leggings to the knee, brass wire gauntlets to the elbow, a crimson spot on her tawny cheek, innumerable necklaces of glass beads on her neck; bizarre things, charms, gifts of witch-men, that hung about her, glittered and trembled at every step. She must have had the value of several elephant-tusks upon her. She was savage and superb, wild-eyed and magnificent; there was something ominous and stately in her deliberate progress. And in the hush that had fallen suddenly upon the whole sorrowful land, the immense wilderness, the colossal body of the fecund and mysterious life seemed to look at her, pensive, as though it had been looking at the image of its own tenebrous and passionate soul. (135–6)

The first two sentences are marked by the constant embellishment and addition of description. This is a stylistic necessity, conveying something of the multiformity that ensures that she, like Kurtz and the wilderness itself, evades Marlow's attempts at definition. Her stateliness – reflected in her 'measured steps' and proud walk with 'head high' – is bolstered by martial images: a 'helmet', 'brass leggings', and 'gauntlets'. But this co-exists with the depiction of her as a contested site through ornamentation that combines the 'barbarous' with colonial commodification: she wears both the 'charms, gifts of witch-men' and 'necklaces of glass beads'. And Marlow's speculation about her ivory adornments exists alongside the striking image of the 'red spot on her tawny cheek'. In summation of the three previous sentences, the fourth, which also begins with the insistent pronoun 'She', contains three contrasted pairs of descriptors, confirming Marlow's struggle to contain the protean nature of this 'apparition'. But it is her apotheosis in the final sentence that is most arresting. Introduced by the conjunction that already suggests their contiguity, it presents her as not merely an emanation of the wilderness, but, in an audacious substitution, 'the image of its own tenebrous and passionate soul'. The degree to which Marlow's narration makes a virtue of vagueness is exemplified in the combination of modalizing locutions, 'seemed' and 'as though', and a shift in register from the tangible to the metaphysical ('soul'), that create semantic conditions whereby the already personified presence of the wilderness is itself reflected in human form. To Marlow, even the woman's gestures seem to make of her a *genius loci*: as she throws up her arms 'as though in an uncontrollable desire to touch the sky', so 'swift shadows darted out on the earth, swept around on the river, gathered the steamer into a shadowy embrace' (136).

True to the rhythms of this narrative, now story now interpretation, now factual now meditative, the focus reverts to the action on the steamboat at this point, where The Harlequin's remarks about the danger posed by the woman provide a demotic contrast to Marlow's mystical interpretation of her. When Marlow overhears some of the conversation taking place in Kurtz's cabin, the reader, placed in an analogous position, infers that Kurtz has seen through the 'philanthropic pretence' of The Manager's rescue mission: 'Save me! – save the ivory, you mean!' (137). This is confirmed when The Manager emerges to tell Marlow that Kurtz has 'done more harm than good to the Company' and that 'trade will suffer'. Ominously, he judges that Kurtz 'did not see the time was not ripe for vigorous action' (137), suggesting that it is not the 'vigorous action' but rather the timing of it that he resents. Kurtz is judged incompetent rather than depraved. To the Manager's claim that Kurtz's methods are 'unsound', Marlow responds that he sees 'No method at all' (137–8), yet when The Manager, seizing the opportunity to dispose of his rival, announces that it is his 'duty to point it out in the proper quarter', Marlow recognizes its true motive and declares that 'Mr. Kurtz is a remarkable man', and instantly becomes *persona non grata*. Instead, he takes comfort in the fact that 'it was something to have at least a choice of nightmares' (138).

Earlier in the narrative, recounting Kurtz's return to the depths of the wilderness, Marlow had pondered his reasons for not returning to the Central Station: 'Perhaps he was just simply a fine fellow who stuck to his work for its own sake' (90). Now, Marlow's dream lies in tatters: Kurtz, his last hope for redeeming the colonial mission, has been revealed to be the epitome of European brutality; and yet Marlow allies himself with this 'nightmare' rather than that represented by the pilgrims. His allegiance to this nightmare resembles the choice he made earlier, between the evident barbarity of the heads on stakes and the rituals of abasement performed before Kurtz (131–2). In this instance, too, he judges the flagrance of Kurtz's depravity preferable to the insidious machinations of the Company agents masquerading as respectability. Having earlier confessed, 'I hate, detest, and can't bear a lie' (82), in making his choice of nightmares, Marlow is being consistent.

Fearing for his safety, The Russian Harlequin departs, but not before Marlow has provided his 'brother seaman' (138) with rifle-cartridges, tobacco, and a new pair of shoes. Whether intended as an interpretive cue or not, shoes loom large in Marlow's adventure: describing how he took over from his predecessor, Fresleven, he uses the commonplace 'stepped into his shoes' (54); he throws his blood-filled shoes into the river after the death of the helmsman; and, now, he bestows a pair of shoes upon the young Russian. A more fruitful echo occurs when The Harlequin explains how he will make his departure, in 'a canoe with three black fellows' (139). Conjuring up the same sense of intrepidity as that of Kurtz, turning his back upon the Central Station to journey back into the wilderness, the image simultaneously sustains the trope of adventure, in which European castaways reinvent themselves in exotic climes, and confirms the Russian as Kurtz's 'disciple'. Naive though it sounds, The Harlequin's claim that Kurtz 'enlarged my mind' (140) is significant, not simply because this narrative can be read as a psychological journey, but also because Kurtz's subjects – love (127) and poetry (140) – invest him with a sensitivity and depth that is simply denied to the other Europeans, who are reduced to mere Company functionaries.

In its disrupted presentation, The Harlequin's revelation that Kurtz ordered the attack on the steamboat conveys something of the contradictory forces exerting their sway upon him and the difficulty of understanding these: 'He hated sometimes the idea of being taken away – and then again. . . . But I don't understand these matters.' Even more importantly, and in an assumption of responsibility to which his narrative testifies and which might be said to provide its rationale, in response to The Harlequin's fears, Marlow assures him: 'Mr. Kurtz's reputation is safe with me' (139). And having elected to be the keeper of Kurtz's reputation, Marlow quickly finds himself called upon to act out his custodial duties. Against a backdrop of the 'uneasy vigil' kept by Kurtz's 'adorers' on the shore, and lulled by the 'narcotic effect' of their 'weird incantations' (140–1), Marlow wakes from a doze to discover Kurtz's cabin empty. Despite his 'moral shock', Marlow exhibits his loyalty 'to the nightmare' of his 'choice' by disembarking from the steamboat alone to pursue 'this shadow'. Thus, the rescue of the ailing Kurtz by The Manager, and the reason for Marlow's presence in Africa, entails this further rescue: the rescue of Kurtz from himself.

Reduced to crawling on all fours, Kurtz leaves a clear trail that Marlow can follow, and he easily overtakes his quarry, this 'vapour exhaled by the earth'. Among his 'imbecile thoughts' at the time is the memory of the old knitter in the Company offices whom he regards as 'a most improper person to be sitting at the other end of such an affair' (142). None the less, invoking her at this point reinforces the metaphorical density of the sequence as Marlow presents Kurtz's motives for escaping in terms of supernatural possession. Within the novella's symbolic frame of reference, Kurtz both reflects the wilderness and is its victim. Standing within thirty yards of the nearest fire, which is attended by 'Some sorcerer, some witch-man' wearing antelope horns, Marlow warns Kurtz – now described as 'that Shadow' and 'this wandering and tormented thing' – that returning to the wilderness will render him 'lost ... utterly lost'. This flash of inspiration has its effect, as Kurtz responds, wistfully, and significantly in the past tense: 'I had immense plans.' And even while recognizing that Kurtz 'could not have been more irretrievably lost', Marlow realizes that the enduring 'foundations of our intimacy were being laid' (143).

The encounter is presented not as a physical meeting between two men, but rather as a tussle between Marlow and the spectral presence of the wilderness to which Kurtz has succumbed, 'the heavy, mute spell ... that seemed to draw him to its pitiless breast by the awakening of forgotten and brutal instincts, by the memory of gratified and monstrous passions' (144). In one formulation, Marlow is in contest with the wilderness for Kurtz's soul. But complicating this is the fact that the untamed energies of the wilderness offer a symbolic representation of this soul, meaning that the 'spell' that bewitches Kurtz is the encounter with his own unchecked and gratified desires that, once indulged, place him beyond the constraints and definition of conventional social forces such as morality: 'I could not appeal in the name of anything high or low. I had, even like the niggers, to invoke him – himself – his own exalted and terrible degradation. There was nothing either above or below him, and I knew it. He had kicked himself loose of the earth' (144). Despite the proclaimed identification, Marlow's terminology serves to confirm the racial stereotyping of colonialism. But this is not really the point here. Instead, revealing its true subject, the narrative interrogates human identity, its scope and limits, and, by extension, the necessary protocols of social cohesion. On another level, there's a continuing discourse about 'them' and 'us' – and the universal setting up of social/racial/cultural boundaries less porous at the time than now: Marlow seeks to reclaim Kurtz for 'us', disallowing his immersion in 'them'.

The figure of Kurtz has been interpreted as an emanation of 'evil'. In this formulation, Conrad's audacity in the novella includes giving new emphasis to the concept of evil by placing it at the centre of Western colonialism, the great contemporary fact of European life at the time of writing. The word 'evil' occurs only three times in the text, most forcefully when linked to 'the profound darkness' (92) at the heart of the wilderness. A more prominent repetition is that of the word 'devil', which, together with its variants 'devilry' and 'devilish', occurs twenty times (slightly fewer than 'darkness', which appears some twenty-five times in the novella). Its contiguity with phrases such as 'witch-craft' and 'witch-men' reminds the reader that the most dramatic way in which the Devil was thought to intervene in human affairs was to be conjured up by witchcraft, as, say, by Faust. Kurtz thus becomes an embodiment of the demonic, conjured up through the practice of witchcraft to take 'a high seat amongst the devils of the land' (116).

Explaining his verdict on Kurtz – 'his soul was mad' – Marlow also identifies the journey undertaken in the novella as an odyssey of self-discovery: 'Being alone in the wilderness, it had looked within itself, and, by heavens! I tell you, it had gone mad. I had – for my sins, I suppose – to go through the ordeal of looking into it myself' (145). Through Kurtz, Marlow comes to understand something of the extremes of human nature beyond the purview of his own lived experience. The sequence gestures forward to Kurtz's final words, trying to summarize his own 'fascination with the abomination' while also replicating its illimitable nature in terms of the story's structural development.

As the steamboat departs, Kurtz's followers – 'two thousand eyes' – follow the progress of 'the fierce river-demon beating the water with its terrible tail' (145), their murmurs 'like the responses from some satanic litany' (146). However crass the attempt to portray the natives' perspective through the technique of defamiliarization, it is consistent with and no less authentic than Marlow's own attempts to explain the mysterious nature of this 'furthest point of navigation' that is simultaneously 'the culminating point' of his experience (51). Furthermore, he proves his sympathies when, recognizing the 'jolly lark' anticipated by the armed pilgrims, he pulls the ship's whistle to frighten the natives away, leaving only the 'barbarous and superb' woman unflinching and stretching 'tragically her bare arms after us over the sombre and glittering river' (146). Whether she survives the valedictory 'fun' is left unclear.

The journey downriver begins with the words: 'The brown current ran swiftly out of the heart of darkness, bearing us down towards the sea.' The current is quickly associated with Kurtz, whose life is described as 'ebbing out of his heart into the sea of inexorable time' (147). Aboard, Marlow finds himself increasingly shunned by the pilgrims and conjoined into an 'unforeseen partnership' with Kurtz, 'this choice of nightmares forced upon me in the tenebrous land invaded by these mean and greedy phantoms' (147). The description of the pilgrims as 'phantoms', extends to them the designation formerly applied to Kurtz – and, naturally, their complicity in the atrocities visited on Africa. Although they are interrupted by his own professional duties and presented fragmentarily or in summary form, Marlow is the recipient of Kurtz's deathbed reflections, the 'shadowy images' that haunt the 'weary wastes of his brain'. In large part, childish megalomania characterizes the memories and dreams that flow into each other and which, if they expose the vanity of human wishes, also testify, as Marlow recognizes, to the struggle of an individual with human nature: 'both the diabolic love and the unearthly hate of the mysteries it had penetrated fought for the possession of that soul satiated with primitive emotions, avid of lying fame, of sham distinction, of all the appearances of success and power' (147–8). The disruptive implications of this encounter can be expressed in the rhetorical question posed in T. S. Eliot's 'Gerontion': 'After such knowledge, what forgiveness?'

Aware that his end is near, Kurtz entrusts Marlow with his private papers. When his final words come, their shocking force lies in their stark simplicity. As Marlow notices on his 'ivory face' the contested expression 'of sombre pride, of ruthless power, of craven terror – of an intense and hopeless despair', Kurtz cries out: 'The horror! The horror!' (149). Wrung from Kurtz at this 'supreme moment of complete knowledge', these words carry annihilatory force for Marlow: 'No eloquence could have been so withering to one's belief in mankind as his final burst of sincerity' (145). The contrast between Marlow's impressions of Kurtz and those of the other Europeans is bald: like his burial the following day, 'in a muddy hole', the announcement of Kurtz's death, by The Manager's servant and in a tone of 'scathing contempt', confirms his standing among the pilgrims: 'Mistah Kurtz – he dead' (150). But Marlow's earlier description of Kurtz's resting place – 'in the mould of primeval earth' (147) – seems more apposite in view of the atavistic terms in which his fall has been couched.

Kurtz's final words have exercised readers. Are they a comment upon Africa and the Africans, resonant with his desire to 'Exterminate all the brutes!' (118)? Are they a comment upon his own potential, manifest in the excesses we have witnessed? Neither of these seems adequate: the first because the phrase haunts Marlow's subsequent visit to Kurtz's fiancée, The Intended, and hence transcends the circumstances of its utterance; and the second because it simply restates the obvious. Nor are these readings endorsed by Marlow's comments that follow, while defending his 'loyalty' and casting it in terms of destiny, he interprets Kurtz's cry as a moral judgement. To begin with, Marlow observes of life that it is 'droll': 'that mysterious arrangement of merciless logic for a futile purpose. The most you can hope from it is some knowledge of yourself – that comes too late – a crop of inextinguishable regrets' (150). This leads to speculation about whether one can pronounce upon it adequately, and he confesses himself humiliated by the fact 'that probably I would have nothing to say' while Kurtz is 'a remarkable man' precisely because 'He had something to say' (151). Not only does Marlow claim that Kurtz 'had summed up – he had judged. "The horror!"' – but he also views this summing-up as 'an affirmation, a moral victory paid for by innumerable defeats, by abominable terrors, by abominable satisfactions' (151). In other words, even in the depths of his degradation, Kurtz has preserved a sense of moral judgement, thereby ensuring Marlow's loyalty: 'But it was a victory! That is why I have remained loyal to Kurtz to the last, and even beyond' (151).

A remarkable transformation has thus occurred in Marlow's narrative. His journey deeper and deeper into Africa proved an odyssey of disenchantment, progressively exposing the brute and brutal nature of his fellow 'civilized' Europeans; his encounter with Kurtz then dashed his last hope to salvage something of his former naive assumptions. But Kurtz's final 'moral victory' over the degradation to which he has surrendered and epitomizes offers him something redemptive: a grain of enduring moral sense, to take away with him from the experience. Kurtz is, ultimately, all the more remarkable for discovering this redemptive possibility in the depths of degradation, beyond the reach of the pilgrims or Marlow who cannot follow him 'over the threshold of the invisible' (151). With Kurtz's death, Marlow's mission to rescue him might be said to end in failure, or at least be qualified. Instead, what has been recovered is Kurtz's legacy. That this, philosophical, adventure is the novella's true journey is proved by the fact that the action reverts to Europe, where Marlow 'found himself back in the sepulchral city' (152), attended by illness, a personal legacy of his travels and a physical expression of the moral shock to which he has been subjected.

His state of delirium supports his vision of his fellow Europeans whose knowledge of life he views as 'an irritating pretence' (152). To Marlow, 'civilized' Europe has become an idea unsupported by any substance. In this manner, his initial comment about colonialism – 'What redeems it is the idea only' (51) – is broadened to include the state of Europe itself. Visited by a Company official wanting Kurtz's papers on the grounds that his knowledge 'of unexplored regions must have been necessarily extensive and peculiar', Marlow counters that this knowledge does not bear 'upon the problems of commerce or administration' (153) and offers him Kurtz's report, having torn off the postscript, which he declines. A second visitor is Kurtz's cousin, who carries away family papers, and a third a journalist, the report's eventual recipient. Each visitor contributes his mite to the vision of Kurtz – 'great abilities'; 'essentially a great musician'; 'proper sphere ought to have been politics' (153, 154) – which in the light of Marlow's knowledge now seems hopelessly inadequate. Even as 'All Europe contributed to the making of Kurtz' (117), so, as these representatives of commerce, family and the press demonstrate, all Europe stakes a claim on his legacy. In a closing tour de force, Marlow's narrative ends with his visit to Kurtz's Intended, to return private letters and her photograph, the last of Kurtz's belongings in his possession.

Marlow's encounter with The Intended is all but overmastered by the attendant memories of Kurtz, creating a reciprocal relationship between the present moment and his past experience. In this manner, Kurtz's pervasive influence is sustained as the narrative past surrounds rather than is succeeded by the narrative present, providing a further illustration of how the novella's psychological tone depends upon fluctuating between foreground and background. Even as Marlow approaches the house at dusk, in a street 'as still and decorous as a well-kept alley in a cemetery', he is assailed by a vision of Kurtz: 'The vision seemed to enter the house with me – the stretcher, the phantom-bearers, the wild crowd of obedient worshippers, the gloom of the forests, the glitter of the reach between the murky bends, the beat of the drum, regular and muffled like the beating of a heart – the heart of a conquering darkness. It was a moment of triumph for the wilderness, an invading and vengeful rush which, it seemed to me, I would have to keep back alone for the salvation of another soul' (155–6). Marlow recalls, and quotes from, a conversation with Kurtz, concerning ownership of the ivory he has collected, in which he said: 'I want no more than justice' (156). Confronting the reader is the task of determining whether Marlow, who seems to hear the 'whispered cry, "The horror! The horror!"' as he enters, does 'justice' to Kurtz in this climactic interview.

The drawing room, with its long windows 'like three luminous and bedraped columns', its marble fireplace of 'cold and monumental whiteness', and its grand piano 'like a sombre and polished sarcophagus' (156), offers a germane setting: a sepulchral room within the sepulchral city, the shrine of dutiful mourning, kept by a woman dressed in black. The impression gains from the appearance of The Intended, pale-faced and still wearing mourning, even though a year has passed since news of Kurtz's death. So powerful are his memories that, to Marlow, the temporal boundaries between Kurtz's death and the mourning fiancée appear to have collapsed: 'I saw her and him in the same instant of time – his death and her sorrow – I saw her sorrow in the very moment of his death' (157). In the claustrophobic atmosphere, in which 'with every word spoken the room was growing darker' (158), such chronological deceit insinuates the presence of Kurtz: in that haven of bourgeois respectability, the drawing room, the sound of The Intended's 'low voice' is palimpsestically overlaid on other sounds 'full of mystery, desolation, and sorrow' emanating from the 'triumphant darkness' from which, Marlow confesses, 'I could not have defended her – from which I could not even have defended myself' (159).

Essentially, their interview represents the individual trials of loyalty to two different images of Kurtz. To The Intended, alone in the world since the recent death of Kurtz's mother, it is an opportunity to confirm that she has proved 'worthy of him' (158). When she puts out her arms 'as if after a retreating figure', she recalls Kurtz's African mistress to Marlow's mind: 'I shall see this eloquent phantom as long as I live, and I shall see her, too, a tragic and familiar Shade, resembling in this gesture another one, tragic also, and bedecked with powerless charms, stretching bare brown arms over the glitter of the infernal stream, the stream of darkness' (160–1). Their shared gestures thus provoke not a comparison but a contrast between the two women: the one, standing defiantly beside the flowing river and surrounded by the jungle, emblematic of the wilderness's energies to which Kurtz surrendered; the other, in the gathering darkness of a room that resembles a mausoleum, symptomatic of the faked authorization of Europe for the colonialism Kurtz represented. The contrast between the two women extends the theme of restraint overwhelmed by desire. Kurtz's journey into the wilderness, and the knowledge he gains there, acquires a sexual dimension, as might be expected from a descent into the human id. Famously, Freud described adult female sexuality as a 'dark continent' for psychology.

The scene reaches its climax when Marlow inadvertently admits to hearing Kurtz's last words and The Intended asks him to repeat them, desiring 'something – something – to – to live with': 'I was on the point of crying to her, "Don't you hear them?" The dusk was repeating them in a persistent whisper all around us, in a whisper that seemed to swell menacingly like the first whisper of a rising wind. "The horror! the horror!" ' But the answer that Marlow gives is a lie:

> 'The last word he pronounced was – your name.'
>
> I heard a light sigh and then my heart stood still, stopped dead short by an exulting and terrible cry, by the cry of inconceivable triumph and of unspeakable pain. 'I knew it – I was sure!' (161–2)

The Intended's 'light sigh' mingling certainty and relief, is all but drowned out by the cry, 'exulting and terrible', that accompanies Marlow as he leaves the house. Why Marlow lies to The Intended is ambiguous. For instance, lying is against his stated principles, yet here it allows him to keep his word to The Harlequin to safeguard Kurtz's reputation; similarly, while preserving The Intended's illusions – and thus sparing her pain – it has also been construed as patronizing in its suggestion that she could not cope with the truth. But who could stand such a truth, and who have the right to deliver it? Marlow certainly has no right to give it to her, and he sees that. The suspicion is that the issue needs to be addressed from another angle. Might it not be seen as an act of kindness, rather? True, it is double-edged, since it involves going against his principles, but the moment reveals how principles are sufficient in the abstract – for instance, the belief that people should not eat each other – but come unstuck in the face of lived reality.

Despite his qualms, Marlow makes good his 'escape', observing that 'The heavens do not fall for such a trifle', but ending his narrative on a note both speculative and justificatory: 'Would they have fallen, I wonder, if I had rendered Kurtz that justice which was his due? Hadn't he said he wanted only justice? But I couldn't. I could not tell her. It would have been too dark – too dark altogether. . . ' (162). While this story of Kurtz transcends the moment of its telling, becoming a myth of man's latent potential for evil, Marlow himself is, necessarily, of his moment and so part of the deception that characterizes Europe. Caught between the nightmares of secrecy and revelation, Marlow's experience suggests that deceptions are necessary in order to survive: they are part and parcel of human existence, as shown when the Africans allow themselves to believe that Kurtz is a god. Here, Marlow bestows a saving illusion. He knows it's an illusion but that's all he's got to give or has the right to give. Typical of the rigorous scepticism of Modernist narrative, the novella troubles a blithe acceptance of absolute morality. Instead, it suggests, hard and fast rules don't work in life. Conrad says this with infinite subtlety across the text, but the end conveys the rottenness of the situation while conceding that we aren't angels. By analogy, in *The Wild Duck*, Ibsen suggests that people are dependent upon 'life lies' in order to cope with the pressures of day-to-day existence.

Marlow's lie is consonant with the falsehood he finds himself surrounded by, and accounts for some of the testamentary nature of his narrative. If his experiences have taught him anything, it is that 'civilized' Europe is an idea whose substance is questionable, founded on illusory absolute moral integrity. In part at least, it is a sham which cannot be admitted, and recognizing this, as Marlow does, involves courage and strength: the realization of the abyss and the will, none the less, to continue living. Marlow's last act is one of compassion and of understanding the limits of his knowledge. Complicatedly, while preserving The Intended's illusions – and the question of whether she would or could believe 'the truth' remains – Marlow's loyalty to Kurtz's memory, the 'nightmare' of his choice, suggests an allegiance to the truth of human nature, however dark.

The novella concludes where it started, aboard the *Nellie*, with Marlow sitting apart, 'in the pose of a meditating Buddha' (162). All that is offered by way of response to the tale, besides the Director's observation that the tide has already begun to ebb, is the frame-narrator's final atmospheric sentence: 'The offing was barred by a black bank of clouds, and the tranquil waterway leading to the uttermost ends of the earth flowed sombre under an overcast sky – seemed to lead into the heart of an immense darkness' (162). And this description itself returns to the imagery that characterized his opening paragraphs. The narrative appears to be circular: beginning and ending on the Thames, just as Marlow's African adventure starts and ends in 'the sepulchral city', and his mission to rescue Kurtz involves a journey up- and then downriver. But something has changed, for Marlow's is a journey from which European civilization's sense of itself does not return intact. The compositional pattern of 'return' thus needs to be seen not as a reversion to a prior state but in the transformative sense that T. S. Eliot describes in 'Little Gidding': 'We shall not cease from exploration / And the end of our exploring / Will be to arrive where we started / And know the place for the first time.'

QUESTIONS

1. Examine the varied presentation of setting in *Heart of Darkness*.
2. In what ways and to what purpose does the narrative of *Heart of Darkness* mimic the literal river-journey that is its subject?
3. Although Kurtz is the object of Marlow's quest in *Heart of Darkness*, his appearance in the novella is delayed and brief. Discuss the effectiveness of this.

CHAPTER 4

CRITICAL RECEPTION AND PUBLISHING HISTORY

COMPOSITION AND PUBLICATION

Begun in December 1898 and finished in February 1899, 'The Heart of Darkness' first appeared in serial form in *Blackwood's Edinburgh Magazine* (vol. 165). It was published in three monthly instalments of *Maga*, as the magazine was familiarly known, between February and April 1899 (pp. 193–200; 479–502; 634–57) that correspond to the novella's tripartite division. Auspiciously, the February 1899 issue was *Maga*'s thousandth number. Three years later the tale, now titled simply *Heart of Darkness*, was incorporated in *Youth: A Narrative and Two Other Stories* (Edinburgh and London: Blackwood, 1902). Conrad's initial conception of this volume as a trilogy of tales narrated by Marlow was thwarted when the third tale (after 'Youth' and *Heart of Darkness*), *Lord Jim*, ran away with him during composition and expanded into a full-length novel, published separately in October 1900. It was replaced in the *Youth* volume by a non-Marlow narrative, 'The End of the Tether'. What survives of the original manuscript of *Heart of Darkness* is housed in the Beinecke Rare Book and Manuscript Library, Yale University, while a fragmentary typescript is held in the Berg Collection, the New York Public Library.

In a letter to William Blackwood of 31 December 1898, Conrad described the story as 'a narrative after the manner of *Youth* told by the same man dealing with his experiences on a river in Central Africa. ... The title I am thinking of is "*The Heart of Darkness*" but the narrative is not gloomy. The criminality of inefficiency and pure selfishness when tackling the civilizing work in Africa is a justifiable idea. The subject is of our time distinc[t]ly – though not topically treated' (*CL*2: 139–40). To David Meldrum, literary adviser in *Blackwood's* London office, Conrad wrote on 2 January 1899 that the tale 'would stand dividing into two instalments' (*CL*2: 145). But, as so often with Conrad, the tale took on a life of its own during composition as new possibilities suggested themselves, and he confessed to Blackwood four days later: 'It has grown upon me a bit' (*CL*2: 147).

BLACKWOOD'S AUDIENCE

The novella's first audience was the readership of *Blackwood's Magazine*. Conrad's association with the monthly began with the publication of 'Karain: A Memory', in November 1897, ended with 'The End of the Tether', in December 1902, and included the Marlow trilogy of 'Youth', *Heart of Darkness*, and *Lord Jim*. He recalled his 'Blackwood's period' with fondness, claiming in 1911: 'One was in decent company there and had a good sort of public. There isn't a single club and messroom and man-of-war in the British Seas and Dominions which hasn't its copy of Maga – not to speak of all the Scots in all parts of the world' (*CL*4: 506). Quite consciously imperialist, and founded in July 1817 as a Tory alternative to the *Edinburgh Review*, *Blackwood's* was, according to Jocelyn Baines, 'a conservative, traditionalist magazine that liked to give its readers good fare in masculine storytelling' (1960: 281). The first audience for *Heart of Darkness* was, thus, conservative in its politics and broadly supportive of Empire. Flattering William Blackwood, the editor and grandson of the magazine's founder, Conrad described himself as '"*plus royaliste que le roi*" – more conservative than Maga' (*CL*2: 162).

One of *Blackwood's* readers was W. L. Alden, an American journalist and short-story writer living and working in London. Alden wrote a regular 'London Literary Letter' to *The New York Times Book Review* from 1898 to 1904. Besides providing his developing opinion of *Heart of Darkness* as it appeared in monthly instalments, his comments also provide a sense of how, even at this early stage of his career, Conrad was being marketed to the American public. On 11 March 1899, Alden, already a devotee of Conrad's writing, described the first instalment as 'full of promise' and ventured that he would be 'very much surprised if [the story] does not justify all that I have ever said of Mr. Conrad' (160). He follows this on 6 May 1899 with the claim that *Heart of Darkness* will mark 'a very decided advance' on Conrad's earlier work, *An Outcast of the Islands* (1896), *The Nigger of the 'Narcissus'* (1897), and *Tales of Unrest* (1898), which already proved that Conrad has 'arrived' and placed him 'among the most original writers of the day'. And Alden prophesies that 'when *Heart of Darkness* comes to be published in book form the public may find that there is more in Mr. Conrad than has hitherto been supposed' (304). Finally, on 17 June 1899, Alden claimed that 'If there are two story writers of the present day who are sure of immortality, Mr. Conrad is one of them' (388) – the other, presumably, Kipling, whom Alden also admired.

Apart from 'Karain', all of Conrad's tales to appear in *Blackwood's* were written with publication in *Maga* in mind and therefore represent his early negotiation of his identity as a writer and his sense of audience. Marlow's Englishness also complicates the relationship between Conrad and his readership for, according to John Galsworthy, 'though English in name', he is 'not so in nature' (1927: 78). Marlow's audience remains the same in 'Youth' and *Heart of Darkness* and, including the Director of Companies, The Accountant and The Lawyer, is generally seen to represent a typical cross-section of the *Blackwood's* readership. Furthermore, while felicitously mimicking Conrad's own insider–outsider status in English letters, the use of a frame-narrator in these stories exploits and dramatizes the relationship between the text and its readers. This technique also had interpretive consequences for a late-nineteenth century audience fed upon a diet of imperial adventure tales. As *Heart of Darkness* demonstrates, Conrad's genius was to transform this genre and interrogate its underlying assumptions. In the novella, frame-narration offers a stylistic expression of cultural boundaries and ideological differences, used to provide an imperial and ironic frame for the story.

CONTEMPORARY REVIEWS AND EARLY CRITICISM

The contemporary reception of the *Youth* volume, published on 13 November 1902, was influenced in its critical direction by an unsigned review by Conrad's friend and early mentor Edward Garnett in *Academy and Literature* (6 December 1902: 606). Prior to this, critics had concentrated their energies on 'Youth', seemingly not knowing what to make of *Heart of Darkness*. Even W. L. Alden's review in *The New York Times Book Review* of 13 December 1902 includes the comment: 'The other two stories are excellent, but they are, of course, a little obscured by the proximity of "Youth"' (10). A publisher's reader and critic, Garnett also generously nurtured such talents as D. H. Lawrence and John Galsworthy. Describing the collection as 'an achievement in art that will materially advance' Conrad's reputation, Garnett quickly identified *Heart of Darkness* as 'the high-water mark of the author's talent', a claim he repeats when bringing the review to a close. To illustrate 'why Mr. Conrad's book enriches English literature', he offers an analysis of the story, identifying its subject as 'the deterioration of the white man's *morale*, when he is let loose from European restraint' and calling it a 'psychological masterpiece'. For Garnett, the 'art' of *Heart of Darkness* lies in 'the relation of the things of the spirit to the things of the flesh, of the invisible life to the visible, of the sub-conscious life within us, our obscure motives and instincts, to our conscious actions, feelings and outlook' (*CCH*: 131, 132).

While introducing critical strands that would be picked up by a later generation of readers, the shaping force of Garnett's opinions upon contemporary reviews can be gauged from Conrad's letter to him of 22 December 1902: 'The ruck takes its tone from you. You know how to serve a friend! I notice the reviews as they come in since your article. ... H of D is this and that and the other thing – they aren't so positive because in this case they aren't intelligent enough to catch on to your indications. But anyway it's a high water mark. If it hadn't been for you it would have been, dreary bosh – an incoherent bogie tale. Yes. That note too was sounded only you came just in time' (*CL*2: 468). And if Garnett's peers lacked his 'intelligent' insight, the focus of their criticism of *Youth* was redirected towards *Heart of Darkness*. The reviewer for *Athenaeum* found it 'the most important part of the book' and demanding 'thoughtful attention' from the 'intelligent' reader (*CCH*: 139).

Perhaps inevitably, the novella's style attracted most attention. To one reviewer, in the *Manchester Guardian*, 'Phrases strike the mind like lines of verse', rendering Conrad 'intensely modern'; while another declared that Conrad 'uses the tools of his craft with the fine, thoughtful delicacy of a mediæval clockmaker' and concluded that 'his short stories are not stories at all, but rather concentrated novels' (*CCH*: 135, 137). This same reviewer, in the *Athenaeum*, praised the 'singular fidelity' with which Conrad presented the 'atmosphere in which his characters move and act' (138).

Conrad's narrative method also had its detractors. John Masefield, later to become Poet Laureate, unfavourably compared Conrad with Kipling, Stevenson and Yeats, and described *Heart of Darkness* as 'a cobweb abounding in gold threads. It gives one a curious impression of remoteness and aloofness from its subject' (*CCH*: 142). E. M. Forster would echo this claim in his famous comment that 'the secret casket of [Conrad's] genius contains a vapour rather than a jewel' (1974: 152). Among Conrad's fellow writers, George Gissing had no such qualms: 'Read Conrad's new book,' he urged: 'He is the strongest writer – in every sense of the word – at present publishing in English. Marvellous writing! The other men are mere scribblers by comparison. That a foreigner should write like this, is one of the miracles of literature' (*CCH*: 140). Similarly, in a review article in 1908 John Galsworthy claimed that the volumes Conrad had published by that date were 'the only writing of the last twelve years that will enrich the English language to any great extent' (*CCH*: 206). With the prescience befitting one of the fathers of science fiction, H. G. Wells mentioned *Heart of Darkness* in *When the Sleeper Wakes*, published in the same year as the novella's serialization, as one of the few works of the Victorian era to have survived into the future, when the sleeper finally awakens.

After Conrad's death in 1924 there was, inevitably, some stocktaking. As the novelist Elizabeth Bowen noted in 1936, 'Conrad is in abeyance. We are not clear yet how to rank him; there is an uncertain pause' (*CCH*: 39). But the 1940s would cement Conrad's critical reputation, beginning with John Dozier Gordan's path-breaking analysis of the biographical and textual sources of Conrad's art in *Joseph Conrad: The Making of a Novelist* (1940), a work that marks the beginning of serious academic study of the author. In the following year F. R. Leavis's 'Revaluations: Joseph Conrad' was published, in two instalments, in *Scrutiny* and subsequently reprinted in *The Great Tradition* (1948). The influential Cambridge critic identified Conrad as 'among the very greatest novelists in the language – or any language' (226) and the natural inheritor of the tradition of the English novel that included Jane Austen, George Eliot and Henry James. Leavis identified a Conrad canon, stretching from *Nostromo* (1904) to *The Shadow-Line* (1917), and recognized in the sea fiction the author's commitment to British national traditions, playing down *Heart of Darkness*, which he saw, in a phrase that has echoed through subsequent criticism, as marred by 'adjectival insistence' (177). Broadly agreeing with E. M. Forster's comments about Conrad's obscurity, he argues that terms such as 'inscrutable', 'inconceivable' and 'unspeakable' are overworked to the point where their effect is 'not to magnify but rather to muffle' (177). But while this 'adjectival and worse than supererogatory insistence' tends to 'cheapen the tone', Leavis also contradictorily concedes that they engender the novella's 'overwhelming sinister and fantastic "atmosphere"' (179, 176).

Leavis and the 'practical criticism' he espoused – based upon a detailed 'close reading' of the text – exerted considerable sway over Conrad studies, and English studies generally, across the three decades that followed. In his approach to literary criticism, Leavis inherited and adapted many of the ideas formulated by Matthew Arnold in the previous century. Arnold saw literature as filling the vacuum created by the decline of religion in its presentation of a system of common social values. The study and appreciation of literature are thus intimately linked to the health of society, and critical reading is driven by moral convictions, with the emphasis falling upon the content rather than the form of the work.

MID-CENTURY AND BEYOND

Two equally influential critical studies from across the Atlantic appeared in the late 1950s: Thomas C. Moser's *Joseph Conrad: Achievement and Decline* (1957) and Albert J. Guerard's *Conrad the Novelist* (1958). Colleagues at Stanford University, California, in their respective introductions the two men acknowledge that their ideas were mutually influential. Moser argued that Conrad's creative powers waned after the publication of *Under Western Eyes* in 1911, tracing this decline in large part to the author's increasing preoccupation with the 'uncongenial subject' of love and sexually charged relationships in his subsequent works. To Moser the period of Conrad's 'achievement' lay between 1898 and 1911, a reformulation that includes *Heart of Darkness*. An important shift in critical perspective in both Moser's and Guerard's studies is the attention paid not only to Kurtz but also to Marlow. At a stroke, this extends the tale's interest beyond an exposé of European degeneration in an exotic setting to the destabilizing impact of this on the perceiving consciousness of Marlow himself, described by Leavis as a 'specific and concretely realized point of view' (1948: 183). Both Moser and Guerard reflect the growing influence of Freud upon literary studies during the decade.

As Marlow's role becomes more than that of narrating presence, so his ordeal in the jungle is increasingly seen to mirror the role of the reader attempting to negotiate the text. In this light, the telling becomes as important as the tale, with Marlow's quest for knowledge foregrounding the reading process. Moser's comments about *Lord Jim* thus apply equally to *Heart of Darkness*: 'Conrad's masterly control of the reader's responses is one of the most significant results of his unorthodox methods ... By holding back information and moving forward and backward in time, Conrad catches up and involves the reader in the moral situation, makes the reader's emotions follow a course analogous to that of the characters' (1957: 42). While gesturing towards the psychoanalytic criticism that Guerard would extend, Moser's book also anticipated the multi-dimensional nature of studies that have since ensured Conrad's enduring reputation by identifying the protean nature of the author of *Heart of Darkness*, among them Conrad the moralist, Conrad the psychologist, Conrad the commentator on politics, and Conrad the artist (38).

In time, each of these areas would receive separate and sustained study, as demonstrated by these titles, a tiny handful that reflect the growing number of books published about Conrad: *The Political Novels of Joseph Conrad: A Critical Study* (1963), by Eloise Knapp Hay; *Mimesis and Metaphor: An Inquiry into the Genesis and Scope of Conrad's Symbolic Imagery* (1967), by Donald C. Yelton; *Conrad: The Psychologist as Artist* (1968), by Paul Kirschner; *Joseph Conrad: The Making of a Moralist* (1972), by John E. Saveson; and John A. Palmer's *Joseph Conrad's Fiction: A Study in Literary Growth* (1968), the first challenge to Moser's 'achievement-and-decline' thesis. Arguing that Conrad's aesthetic development and experiment was sustained across his career, Palmer's study has influenced a wave of revisionist criticism.

Giving the keynote to his approach, Guerard's study includes discussion of *Heart of Darkness* in a chapter that collects Conrad's autobiographical stories under the heading 'The Journey Within'. Guerard uses psychoanalytical ideas to interpret Marlow's odyssey in *Heart of Darkness* as 'a spiritual voyage of self-discovery', arguing that it constitutes a Jungian 'night journey'. In this reading, Marlow's dreamlike experience involves a confrontation with his own dark nature, the climax of which is provided when he recognizes his kinship with Kurtz, his 'potential and fallen self' (1958: 38). In this reading, which draws upon Edward Garnett's view of the tale as a 'psychological masterpiece', the obscurity that Leavis decried in the method is found to be central to the story's meaning: 'I am willing to grant that the unspeakable rites and unspeakable secrets become wearisome, but the fact – at once literary and psychological – is that they must remain *unspoken*. A confrontation with such a double and facet of the unconscious cannot be reported through realistic dialogue' (42). This is not to suggest that Guerard, nor Moser before him, detaches *Heart of Darkness* from its political and historical contexts, but rather that this interest here serves as a backdrop for the exploration of 'psychic needs', with the emphasis falling upon Marlow's 'symbolic descent into the unconscious' (48). Furthermore, while Guerard's repeated emphasis upon the 'psycho-moral' in *Heart of Darkness* may strike the contemporary reader as archaic in the wake of claims about the 'Death of the Author', it is worth recalling the degree to which Conrad encouraged posterity to bracket the man and the work, referring to *Heart of Darkness* in his 'Author's Note' to *Youth* as: 'experience pushed a little (and only very little) beyond the actual facts of the case' (xi).

Conrad criticism flourished in the decades that followed, with *Heart of Darkness* receiving – and continuing to receive – the lion's share of wide-ranging attention. For instance, stressing the novella's formal qualities, Leo Gurko's *Joseph Conrad: Giant in Exile* (1960) traced meaning in its symmetrical unity, whereby Marlow's lie to The Intended becomes a refashioning of the lie about imperialism. A decade later, Bruce Johnson's *Conrad's Models of Mind* (1971) located the tale within a philosophical tradition that includes Arthur Schopenhauer and Jean-Paul Sartre, and presenting the meaninglessness of experience in terms of a confrontation with existential absurdism. Literary as well as philosophical traditions were invoked to provide a context, as demonstrated by David Thorburn's *Conrad's Romanticism* (1974), with its claims that Marlow's struggles to articulate his experience replicate those of Wordsworth, who confesses in 'Lines Composed a few miles above Tintern Abbey': 'I cannot paint / What then I was.' Biography, too, exploited the novella's potential, with Frederick R. Karl arguing, in *Joseph Conrad: The Three Lives*, that the 'seeming disparity between Marlow's moderation and Kurtz's anarchy' repeats divisions that 'Conrad sensed within himself' (1979: 488). Where an earlier generation of interpreters had used the life to explain the work, a later one used the work to explain the life.

Ian Watt's justly acclaimed study, *Conrad in the Nineteenth Century* (1979), generously places each of Conrad's early works within a host of contexts – biographical, philosophical, scientific and literary – in order to reveal their shaping influences upon Conrad's art. His chapter on *Heart of Darkness* thus relates the novella to its biographical sources before expanding its contextual frame of reference to include the *fin de siècle*, symbolism and Impressionism, the Victorian work ethic and religion of progress, ideologies of imperialism and evolutionary thought. As such, Watt's book engages with and distils two decades of Conrad criticism.

RECENT TRENDS: POLITICS AND GENDER

In the second half of the twentieth century, literary criticism was increasingly driven by what might be termed the 'sociologizing' of a text. This involved applying non-instrinsic political, social and cultural theories to works of literature as literary studies became increasingly theory-driven in the wake of the 'structuralist revolution' in universities in the 1960s and 1970s. Through these and ensuing decades the range of interpretive '-isms' was brought to bear upon *Heart of Darkness*, including Marxism, feminism, post-structuralism and post-colonialism, each seeking to expose inherent power relations within the text, each with its ideological bias that often predetermined the conclusions of its inquiry. Rather than attempting to summarize the shifts within these trends, three illustrative examples here delineate their working methodologies.

Drawing on basic Marxist theories, that view human life as determined by its relationship to the means of economic production, and history as a class struggle, inspired by competition for economic, social and political advantage, critics became increasingly concerned with the underlying political substratum in the novella. Applying Marxist views to literature inevitably leads to politicizing the text. The title of Frederick Jameson's influential book, *The Political Unconscious: Narrative as a Socially Symbolic Act* (1981), succinctly describes the approach. Steve Smith, for instance, begins by identifying a contradiction: the colonial exploitation Marlow encounters in Africa is only such within the context of humanism, the very ideology employed to justify the venture. Marlow's awareness of the workings of the colonial economy, whereby 'rubbishy' trade goods are exchanged for 'a precious trickle of ivory', leads Smith to argue that the narration 'foregrounds that revealing incongruity between rhetoric and the reality of colonialism' (1987: 187). Examining Marlow's economic situation, and the historical forces to which he is subject, leads to the conclusion that his disorientation in the Congo mirrors his status as a displaced ocean-going seafarer: 'Marlow can thus be considered in relation to a whole mode of production that predates the frenzied penetration of the African continent and which is now threatened, or profoundly transformed by its arrival' (189). Thus *Heart of Darkness* is seen to be concerned with what happens when one mode of production and its attendant technologies and ideology is overlaid on another, older one. In this way, the novella invites a critique of the colonial system, and the narrative is seen to be characterized by an implicit unease about the assumptions on which the colonial exploitation is founded. According to Smith, this 'unease' is manifest in the narrative itself rather than in Marlow, whose destruction of the postscript to Kurtz's report, in particular, renders him antagonistic to the unpalatable realities of history and politics.

Although Marxism, possibly in response to world affairs, has declined in popularity, its methods influenced another, more recent ideological approach: New Historicism. Typically, New Historicists juxtapose a literary text with contemporary non-literary texts in order to read the former in terms of the latter and, by treating the two on parity, attempt to read the literary text anew by detaching it from the weight of previous criticism. In this way, reminiscent of Marxism, a dialogue ensues between history and literature in which the work is related to the period of its composition.

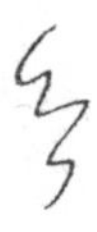

Applying a feminist viewpoint to the, largely, 'man's world' of Conrad's works was timely. Typically dealing with the inherited male preserve, such as colonialism, the British Merchant Service and politics, and endorsing codes of conduct that embraced chivalry, stoicism and scepticism (typically male concerns), the gender bias in his fiction was marked – and markedly of its age. A contemporary reviewer's praise for *The Nigger of the 'Narcissus'* included the comment that 'There is not a petticoat in all Mr. Conrad's pages' (*CCH*: 88). Indebted to a tradition that stretches back as least as far as Mary Wollstonecraft's *A*

Vindication of the Rights of Women (1792), and invigorated by the 'women's movement' of the 1960s, feminist literary criticism questions the assumptions of patriarchy that underpin the presentation of women in literature. By attending closely to the narrative strategies used to disempower women, a feminist reading of a text examines the representation of women in order to expose and challenge the manner in which they are defined, invariably as 'Other', 'absence', or part of 'nature'.

In her reading of *Heart of Darkness*, Johanna M. Smith argues that, when describing Kurtz's African mistress as an embodiment of the jungle, Conrad fuses patriarchy and imperialism: 'As the patriarchal ideology intends with its power of image-making to distance and hence conquer the woman's body, so the imperialist ideology intends with its power for good to distance the mysterious life of the jungle. And both the savage woman and the jungle are momentarily silenced by Marlow's images of them. As these images interrupt the movement of the narrative, however, they create gaps by which the reader can see the impossibility of such ideological containment' (1989: 186).

Drawing on psychoanalysis and reader-response theory, and, in effect, bearing out the fact that the tale was written for *Maga*, Nina Pelikan Straus argues that the novella's artistic conventions are 'brutally sexist' and finds Marlow's narrative aimed at a male 'reader-participator': 'these words are understood differently by feminist readers and by mainstream male commentators.' In this reading, Marlow's lie to The Intended excludes both her and female readers unless they are 'willing to suspend their womanliness far enough to forever dissociate themselves from the women characters' (1987: 125, 129). But Conrad has his defenders, too, among feminist critics. In the first book-length study of his works from a feminist perspective, Ruth L. Nadelhaft asserted that he wrote 'through the critical eyes of his women characters' and that 'Through narrative strategies, female characterizations, and reference to his own marginal status, Conrad found means to express in works prized by patriarchal culture a consistent and profound criticism of that very culture' (1991: 12).

Feminist and post-colonial critiques are founded upon comparable methodologies. Where feminism is gender-oriented, seeking to expose strategies whereby woman is 'othered' within a matrix of patriarchal attitudes, a post-colonial reading focuses upon the 'othering' of race and culture that results from a Eurocentric view of the world, the conscious or unconscious processes by which Europe and European cultural assumptions are accepted as normal, natural and universal. Post-colonial critics also emphasize the politics of representation, arguing that, in the grand narrative of Empire, the colonized are reduced to characters in someone else's story – the story told by the colonizer – and denied a story or voice of their own. As such, they are divested of a cultural heritage. Involving similar modes of subjugation, patriarchy, colonialism, racism and sexism may be conflated to reveal colonialism as a hyper-masculine construct that subordinates not just persons of another colour but also women. With much of it set in the non-European world, it was inevitable that Conrad's writings would attract post-colonial attention, but a cause célèbre in critical circles helped to foster the continuing debate about race and racism.

In a self-consciously polemical lecture delivered at the University of Massachusetts in February 1975, the Nigerian novelist and critic Chinua Achebe accused Conrad of being 'a bloody racist'. The charge was toned down to 'thoroughgoing racist' when the lecture was published in revised form as 'An Image of Africa'. According to Achebe, *Heart of Darkness* – 'an offensive and deplorable book' – offers only a reductive image of Africa, and presents Africans as dehumanized embodiments of evil. As such, they are reduced 'to the role of props for the break-up of one petty European mind', hereby confirming 'the need ... in Western psychology to set Africa up as a foil to Europe, as a place of negations at once remote and vaguely familiar, in comparison with which Europe's own state of spiritual grace will be manifest' (1989: 12,3). In answer to these criticisms, it has been suggested that the subject of the novella is less the confrontation between Europe and Africa, fashioned, as he sees it, in terms of one man's moral and psychological breakdown, than a much broader investigation of the crisis of European identity. Similarly, detaching the novella from the historical contexts in which it was produced results in a wilfully impoverished reading. Some of Marlow's attitudes inevitably seem patronizing to a later audience, but written in an age when imperial Britain was competing for its share of African territory, the condemnation of racial exploitation in *Heart of Darkness* was for its time bravely interrogative and ideologically subversive. 'Presentism', whereby the past is judged guilty by today's lights, ill serves the understanding of highly complex phenomena.

Achebe's challenge to the comfortable reading of the novella, as an attack against racism, has probably provoked more critical debate than any other single piece of Conrad criticism. He has received support and censure, from both European and non-European critics. The Ugandan writer, Peter Nazareth, for instance, argues that far from validating racist views the narrative demonstrates the erosion of Marlow's 'inherited racist framework through the direct experience of Africa, through reflection on that experience, and through the telling of the story'. And Nazareth goes so far as to suggest that Achebe's hostility to *Heart of Darkness* is itself symptomatic of a post-colonial attitude: 'the explanation is that once Conrad helped colonials break out, some of them looked back and found him unnecessary' (1983: 177, 182). Among recent full-length monographs, mention must be made of Peter Edgerly Firchow's *Envisioning Africa: Racism and Imperialism in Conrad's 'Heart of Darkness'* (1999), which, historical and contextual in approach, examines the discrepancy between late Victorian and contemporary usages of such terms as 'race', 'racism' and 'imperialism', and intelligently reveals how blithely equating them results in distortions and misinterpretation. Paradoxically, whatever the validity of his charge, Achebe's criticism has served to ensure that race continues to be a central issue in the ongoing study of this most fascinating of tales and that *Heart of Darkness*, in his own words, 'plagues us still'.

The arc of the novella's critical reception suggests a pendulum swinging back and forth between aesthetics and history. This is probably inevitable, for, like all great works, we simply haven't come to the end of knowing it, and thus each generation finds its varying concerns reflected in it, or not. To its first readership,

Heart of Darkness was certainly a strongly anti-colonialist work, offering a political message against a particular form of economic organization that was found in its most ruthless form in Leopold II's Congo Free State.

In 1903, acting as an agent for the Congo Reform Association, Roger Casement, who met Conrad at Matadi in 1890, appealed to the novelist for assistance, seeing in him a fellow spirit, whose work had passionately cried out against the abuses then current. A year later, the Association's founder, E. D. Morel, in his *King Leopold's Rule in Africa* (1904), quoted a letter that Conrad wrote to Casement: 'seventy five years or so after the abolition of the slave trade (because it was cruel) there exists in Africa a Congo State, created by the act of European Powers where ruthless systematic cruelty towards the blacks is the basis of administration, and bad faith towards all other states the basis of commercial policy' (*CL*3: 95). And writing to Conan Doyle on 7 October 1909, a year after the Belgian government had annexed the territory from their king, Morel described *Heart of Darkness* as 'the most powerful thing ever written on the subject'.

Widely translated, and perennially feted with critical editions and contextualizing studies, *Heart of Darkness* remains a staple of university courses and on the reading list of the serious reader. That its fortunes continue to be debated is testament to its fascination, while bearing out the author's fashioning of the ancient claim of *Ars longa, vita brevis*:

> No secret of eternal life for our books can be found amongst the formulas of art, any more than for our bodies in a prescribed combination of drugs. This is not because some books are not worthy of enduring life, but because the formulas of art are dependent upon things variable, unstable and untrustworthy; on human sympathies, on prejudices, on likes and dislikes, on the sense of virtue and the sense of propriety, on beliefs and theories that, indestructible in themselves, always change their form – often in the lifetime of one fleeting generation.
>
> ('Books', *Notes on Life and Letters* 5–6)

QUESTIONS

1. The critical reception of *Heart of Darkness* reveals uncertainty about whether Kurtz or Marlow is at the centre of the narrative. What is your view? Support your answer with illustrative quotations from the novella.
2. *Heart of Darkness* has been subjected to a range of critical approaches, including biographical, psychoanalytical, Marxist, feminist, and post-colonial. Briefly trace the findings of these approaches and decide upon their usefulness.
3. Chinua Achebe famously described Conrad as a 'bloody racist' on the basis of *Heart of Darkness*. What *textual* evidence do you find in the novella (a) to support this charge; and, (b) to refute it?

CHAPTER 5

ADAPTATION, INTERPRETATION AND INFLUENCE

THE QUESTION OF INFLUENCE

In *Heart of Darkness*, Conrad fashioned a myth about the unpalatable side of human nature with which he struck a chord that resonates yet. The title itself has become a media byword for atrocity. According to Sven Lindqvist: 'Everywhere in the world where knowledge is being suppressed, knowledge that, if it were made known, would shatter our image of the world and force us to question ourselves – everywhere there, *Heart of Darkness* is being enacted' (1997: 172). Lindqvist titled his study of European involvement in Africa, fashioned as a travelogue recounting his journey across the Sahara, *Exterminate All the Brutes*, after the 'valuable postscriptum' to Kurtz's report.

Alongside its artistic influence, one indicator of how *Heart of Darkness* has entered the language is the degree to which it pervades popular discourse. The story continues to be subjected to widespread adaptation and parodic treatment. For instance, an episode of the popular television programme *The Simpsons* was punningly entitled *Bart of Darkness*. In another episode, 'Kiss Kiss, Bang Bangalore', whose title is a nod to the film *Kiss Kiss, Bang Bang* (2005), Homer travels to India in order to train new employees, but becomes power-crazed in his new position of authority and, by the time he is 'rescued', has assumed godlike status. Similarly, *Star Trek: Insurrection* (1998) drew plot inspiration from *Heart of Darkness*. A recent study of Gothic literature by Anne Williams is titled *Art of Darkness* (1995). Trivial in themselves, perhaps, these playful examples are testaments to the widespread recognition of *Heart of Darkness*.

A successful literary parody depends upon an understanding of the original's meaning and method. Conrad's early style, 'Conradese' as he himself called it (*CL*1: 301), and early subject matter were quickly parodied. Max Beerbohm's parody of the 'The Lagoon' in *A Christmas Garland* (1912) is both amusing and a form of homage. And Conrad confessed himself 'most agreeably guyed' (*Tales of Unrest*: vi) by the result.

The issue of artistic influence, and thus the art of adaptation, is a complex one. A work of art does not exist in a vacuum. Rather, it is necessarily in dialogue with other works of art, whether to confirm or react against their standards. As T. S. Eliot noted in 'Tradition and the Individual Talent' (1919): 'No poet, no artist of any art, has his complete meaning alone. His significance, his appreciation is the appreciation of his relation to the dead poets and artists' (1980: 15). In this way, the 'meaning' of *Heart of Darkness* is partly determined by its relationship to other late-nineteenth century writings about colonialism by authors such as Kipling, Stevenson and Haggard. But, equally, a work of art's uniqueness is determined by its ability to escape the dominance of influence. Conrad, for instance, resisted critical attempts to pigeonhole him, whether shrugging off comparisons with Kipling or baulking at the 'sea writer' tag his early fiction attracted.

The artist is caught in a dilemma between adherence to tradition, on the one hand, and the need to evade this, on the other. To Harold Bloom this amounts to an Oedipal struggle that he describes as 'the anxiety of influence' (1973). Graham Greene exhibits this when he worries about falling under the influence of Conrad's style in *Heart of Darkness*: 'how often he compares something concrete to something abstract. Is this a trick that I have caught?' (1968: 44). Perhaps it is the duty of the artist to say, with Stephen Dedalus in *A Portrait of the Artist as a Young Man* (1916): 'I will not serve' (1968: 243). But where does this leave adaptation, whereby works of art deliberately respond to and are influenced by each other? In *Real Presences* (1989), George Steiner argues that the best interpretation of a work of art is not a detached critical essay but a 'vitalizing assessment' (13) of the text. So, he argues, the critical interpretation of a Beethoven piano sonata is to be found in but a performance of it. Similarly, the best way to 'analyse' Homer's *Odyssey* is to re-write it – as James Joyce does in *Ulysses*.

As Cedric Watts puts it: 'The tale's cultural echoes extend through time and across continents' (in Stape ed., 1996: 52). Although the influence of *Heart of Darkness* is most evident in literature, it has inspired and been adapted by other art forms too, and examples from two of these will help to show this.

Heart of Darkness *and the Other Arts*

During a visit to Conrad in 1910, the Virginia pianist and composer, John Powell, suggested that the author consider writing an opera libretto based on *Heart of Darkness*. Conrad's response was to frown and leave the room. He later wrote to Powell to say that 'he believed it would be impossible to put the whole in dramatic form, and suggested that the material might better be used as the theme of a symphonic poem' (Randall ed., 1968: 60 n.). Powell eventually wrote a piece for piano and orchestra entitled *Rhapsodie nègre*. Dedicated 'To Joseph Conrad in appreciation of and gratitude for *Heart of Darkness*', it premièred at New York's Carnegie Hall in March 1918 and enjoyed considerable success, especially while the composer remained active as a pianist. The music mingles various African and European styles to portray aurally the conflict of cultures described in Conrad's work. A review of a later performance, in 1929, describes the introduction in terms that suggest Powell's attentiveness to the original source: 'The opening wail of the orchestra and the free preluding which lead to the main body of the work have some of the whiff and the blackness of the jungle, and these places return significantly' (Downes, 1929: 32). Although no opera of *Heart of Darkness* has yet been produced, other works by Conrad have been adapted, including *Under Western Eyes*, *Victory* and *Lord Jim*, the last of which won the Prince Pierre de Monaco Prize for the best opera of 1973.

Beginning with the silent film of *Victory* in 1919, nearly ninety films based on Conrad's works had been made by the end of the twentieth century. The problem of converting Conrad's indirect and often ironic narration from the page and onto the screen continues to bedevil film-makers. None the less, among the best of these are Carol Reed's *An Outcast of the Islands* (1952), Terence Young's *The Rover* (1967), Ridley Scott's *The Duellists* (1977) and Francis Ford Coppola's *Apocalypse Now* (1979).

The first attempt to film *Heart of Darkness* is part of cinematic folklore. In 1939, and already famous for his radio broadcasts which included two adaptations of the novella, the 24-year-old Orson Welles was invited to Hollywood by RKO studios, who agreed to sponsor him to make a film of his choosing. He chose *Heart of Darkness*. Casting himself as Kurtz, Welles 'solved' the problem of narration by having the camera, and thus the viewer, play the part of Marlow. The project ran over budget and was never filmed. Instead, Welles brought these creative energies to bear upon his next film, *Citizen Kane* (1941).

Since then there have been various cinematic adaptations of *Heart of Darkness*: two versions appeared in the United States in the 1950s; an Italian version in 1968; a Spanish version in 1978; Nicholas Roeg's version, starring John Malkovich and Tim Roth, in 1994. To these can be added a spoof version, filmed on a shoestring budget and titled *Cannibal Women in the Avocado Jungle of Death* (1988), in which actress and former *Playboy* bunny Shannon Tweed ventures into the 'avocado jungle' of Southern California to rescue 'Dr Kurtz', a radical feminist turned cannibal, played by the Queen of the B-films, Adrienne Barbeau.

Easily the best-known adaptation of *Heart of Darkness*, however, is Coppola's *Apocalypse Now*, which transports Conrad's novella into the Vietnam War. Made six years after the ceasefire that saw the withdrawal of American troops from Vietnam, the film uses the novella's structure, themes and images. To anyone who has read *Heart of Darkness*, *Apocalypse Now* sounds like an echo chamber of the novella as so many of Marlow's words are woven into the film-script. Curiously, the film credits do not mention *Heart of Darkness*. In the film, a Marlow/narrator-figure, Captain Willard (Martin Sheen), is sent to end the reign of a Colonel Walter E. Kurtz (Marlon Brando). He travels up the Nung River with a four-man crew, deep into the jungles of Cambodia, to find 'the Colonel', an unrestrained ego-maniac, deified by his followers, for whom his word is law, and capable of cruelty on a grand scale. The film captures in vivid and brutal detail the mayhem and madness of war, its traumatic and psychological impact upon the soldiers involved, and the steady debasement of human values.

Besides these full-length adaptations, the incidental influence of *Heart of Darkness* pervades cinema. To take just two examples: in Carol Reed's *The Third Man* (1949), based on a novel by Graham Greene, the villain, Harry Lime, played by Orson Welles, exerts a Kurtzian ability to inspire others, while one of his henchmen is named 'Baron Kurtz'; while Werner Herzog's *Aguirre, The Wrath of God* (1972), in which a band of conquistadors travel down the Amazon River in search of El Dorado, offers a sceptical vision of colonialism as mental instability and depravity affect the group the further it travels into the jungle.

CONRAD'S LITERARY INFLUENCE

Conrad's influence upon his contemporaries is obvious. T. S. Eliot originally intended Kurtz's last words as an epigraph to *The Waste Land* (1922), but was dissuaded by Ezra Pound. In the event, he chose those spoken by The Manager's servant, 'Mistah Kurtz – he dead', as the epigraph for his poem 'The Hollow Men' (1925), no doubt influenced by Marlow's description of Kurtz as 'hollow at the core'. Conrad's friend and sometime collaborator, Ford Madox Ford, claimed in a letter of 1920: 'I learned all I know of Literature from Conrad' (Ludwig ed., 1965: 127). While Virginia Woolf, in her essay 'Mr. Bennett and Mrs. Brown' (1924), offered Conrad as an example to be followed by his fellow writers, Arnold Bennett, John Galsworthy and H. G. Wells (1981: 99). One of those who fell under Conrad's spell was George Orwell who, in 1949, described him as 'one of the very few true novelists that England possesses', and claimed that Conrad had 'civilized' English literature by bringing it 'back into contact with Europe' (1978: 555, 551).

Across the Atlantic, the next generation of writers paid homage to his genius. F. Scott Fitzgerald, Ernest Hemingway,

William Faulkner, and Malcolm Lowry all cited his influence. Fitzgerald's use of Nick Caraway as character-narrator in *The Great Gatsby* (1925) was suggested by Conrad's use of Marlow in *Lord Jim*, and Faulkner drew upon Conrad's 1905 essay on Henry James for his Nobel Prize acceptance speech in 1950. Defending Conrad's reputation in 1924, Hemingway irreverently claimed: 'It is agreed by most of the people I know that Conrad is a bad writer, just as it is agreed that T. S. Eliot is a good writer. If I know that by grinding Mr. Eliot into a fine dry powder and sprinkling that powder over Mr. Conrad's grave Mr. Conrad would shortly appear, looking very annoyed at the forced return, and commence writing I would leave for London early tomorrow morning with a sausage grinder' (White ed., 1968: 114).

Conrad's works were also viewed as a *modus vivendi* in times of crisis. In an essay entitled 'The Conrad of my Generation' (1957), Jan Józef Szczepański recalled how the German occupation of Poland in the Second World War 'created the moral climate of a Conrad novel', and how their erstwhile countryman's works provided succour to members of the Polish resistance: 'His books became a collection of practical recipes for men fighting lonely battles in the dark that was dense enough to hide personal defeats and therefore represented an additional challenge' (in Najder ed., 1983: 279).

Conrad's shaping influence on the development of literature endures through techniques that he refined and made his own, such as indirect narration and disrupted chronology, while his universal appeal is evident in the fact that his works have been and continue to be translated into more than forty languages, from Albanian to Yiddish.

THE INFLUENCE OF *HEART OF DARKNESS*

In the year of Conrad's birth, J. M. Ballantyne published *The Coral Island* (1857). The story of three young English boys shipwrecked on a Pacific island was an immediate success. Before their rescue by the English missionary, the boys display the fortitude and civilized qualities of idealized traits of Victorian society, even spreading Christianity to the natives, before returning home. Nearly a century later, William Golding revisited the scenario in *Lord of the Flies* (1954). But in this version, the group of English schoolboys without adult supervision descend into barbarism. By the time of their rescue, any vestige of civilization has been replaced by cruelty, savagery and death. It seems no accident that, lying roughly midway between Ballantyne's optimistic vision and Golding's bleakness, is *Heart of Darkness*, and the degree to which Conrad's vision of human nature threatens any consoling belief in the sustaining force of civilized values outside the restraints of society. Golding's novel ends with Ralph weeping 'for the end of innocence, the darkness of man's heart' (223).

The following discussion offers a representative selection of the literary texts that have responded to *Heart of Darkness* to demonstrate how Conrad's successors, both European and non-European, have responded to the novella's influence; one necessarily imprecise, though it is possible to demonstrate convincing affinities that suggest its presence.

European Responses

An early instance of the novella's influence is provided by Leonard Woolf's 'Pearls and Swine' (1921). Set against the backdrop of pearl fishing in Ceylon, where Woolf had worked in the Colonial Service, it recounts the downfall of a second-rate Kurtz-figure, the alcoholic Mr White. Formal and thematic similarities link the stories. Told by an unnamed narrator to friends in the 'faint civilised aroma of whisky and soda' (in Boehmer ed., 1998: 415) of an English hotel smoking room, Woolf's tale makes use of frame-narration; while in what the narrator terms 'the problem of East and West' (416), the issue of whether White finally succumbs because of the 'hold' (423) exerted by his colonial surroundings or because of his ineffectual 'civilised' personality allies him with his counterpart in *Heart of Darkness*. Woolf was advised to tone down this critical tale of British imperial power for his American market. He refused to do so, and the tale remained unpublished there.

As has been suggested here, Conrad's own adventures in Africa provide the basis of *Heart of Darkness*. His journey in turn inspired later generations of adventurer-writers to follow in his footsteps. A friend of Conrad, the French author, André Gide, who translated and promoted his works in France, visited the Congo and Chad in 1925–6, dedicating his *Voyage au Congo* (1927) to Conrad's memory. In 1959, when researching *A Burnt-out Case* (1961), set in a remote leper colony, Graham Greene visited the Belgian Congo. His 'Congo Journal', published in *In Search of a Character* (1968), records his reading of *Heart of Darkness* for the first time since 'about 1932 because [Conrad's] influence on me was too great and too disastrous. The heavy hypnotic style falls around me again, and I am aware of the poverty of my own' (42). Another book Greene read in the Congo was Romain Gary's *Les Racines du chiel* (1956), whose protagonist he describes as 'A French Marlow' (48). In a subsequent work, *La Nuit sera calme* (1974), Gary offered a provocative observation on Conrad that translates as: 'The English have not yet forgiven him for being without doubt their greatest novelist of this century' (258).

A Burnt-out Case is set shortly before the Congo's independence and recounts the story of Querry, a British architect, whose general lost enthusiasm for life, including his faith, leads him to retire to a 'leproserie', run by Belgian monks and nuns. There, among the 'burnt-out cases' (125) – lepers whose illness has left them mutilated but is no longer active – Querry's zest for life returns, partly thanks to the influence of his servant, Deo Gratias, and he designs a hospital building for the station. Finding himself of service, Querry pronounces himself 'content' (146) and wants to stay at the station for ever: 'I can't go back where I came from, Deo Gratias. I don't belong there any more' (209). A journalist for the *Post*, Parkinson, in the country to cover the independence struggles, finds in Querry a news story and, despite the latter's objections, presents him in the pages of the press as a noble philanthropist: 'An Architect of Souls' (153). The self-promoting reporter, who perceives himself as a latter-day Stanley, tells his readers that he has 'penetrated what Joseph Conrad called the Heart of Darkness' (154). When Mme Rycker, a Belgian woman, falsely accuses Querry of having had sexual relations with her, her husband fatally shoots him. Equally false is the reputation Querry leaves behind him, thanks to Parkinson, who presents him as having gone morally astray in the tropics: 'Death of a Hermit. The Saint who Failed' (235).

From the description on the opening page of the sense of escape that Africa offers Querry – 'like a nut at the centre of the hard shell of discomfort' (1) – to the description of palm nuts waiting to be pressed – 'like dried and withered heads, the product of a savage massacre' (161) – Greene's novel contains subtle reminders of images and ideas in *Heart of Darkness*. Querry himself is described by one of the monks as 'a remarkable man' (93). Where European dereliction is responsible for the decaying machinery in *Heart of Darkness*, in *A Burnt-out Case* an agitator can incite the Africans to destroy imported hospital machinery by spreading rumours that it is intended to torture the patients: 'Yet in our century you could hardly call them fools. Hola Camp, Sharpeville and Algiers had justified all possible belief in European cruelty' (44). In this way, Greene's text sustains and reworks its Conradian influence. Another of Greene's visits, to West Africa in 1941, provided source material for *The Heart of the Matter* (1948). His journal, 'Convoy to West Africa', concludes with a confession that conflates the beginnings of Conrad's (and Marlow's) fascination with the 'dark continent' and the novella that so inspired Greene: 'to me ... Africa will always be the Africa of the Victorian atlas, the blank unexplored continent the shape of the human heart' (1968: 105).

Non-European Responses

In various ways, the examples cited above bear traces of the influence of *Heart of Darkness*. But in each of these examples the vision of Africa is presented by a European author. The publication of Edward Said's *Orientalism* (1978) drew attention to the way in which Western art constructs an image of the non-European world that sustains a colonial vision. Given its influence upon the European vision of Africa, it is inevitable that the writings of African authors should have been cast as a response to the novella. As the now familiar post-colonial cliché has it: the Empire writes back. These writings thus exhibit a different form of the influence of *Heart of Darkness*: by presenting an

Afrocentric vision (though in Western languages), they engage with Conrad's text in a critical dialogue, as though written in its interstices, reacting to the vision it promulgates. As Chinua Achebe has claimed: 'the story we had to tell could not be told for us by anyone else, no matter how gifted and well-intentioned' (1989: 38).

The publication of Achebe's *Things Fall Apart* (1958), its title a quotation from W. B. Yeats's 'The Second Coming', had an immediate impact upon African literature and its reception. Set in Achebe's native Nigeria during the last decade of the nineteenth century, it tells the story of Okonkwo, one of the elders of the Ibo tribe of the village of Umuofia, of his rise to become the head of a prosperous family, his seven-year banishment from the village for killing a clansman, and his eventual suicide when he falls foul of the first British intruders, the missionaries and representatives of government. By this point Okonkwo is convinced that the tribal bonds are weakening to the point where it will not defend itself against this outside influence.

The novel's Conradian echoes include Okonkwo's possession of a human head, a spoil of war, from which he drinks, and a variant on the technique of delayed decoding: using the word 'money' before revealing that the currency is 'cowries' invites the reader to invest the latter with all the connotations of the former which might otherwise have been suspended. But the tale's real significance lies in its presentation of Ibo culture 'from the inside'. The use of proverbs, tribal rituals and traditions, and myths, supported by the rich use of Ibo proverbs and terms, constructs a cultural identity and authenticity that is not present in the Africans in *Heart of Darkness*. The novel's realism invites historical and ideological consideration: it presents a pre-colonial reality that is Ibo-centric – and thus a challenge to a Eurocentric colonial reality. The novel thus defines itself against the District Commissioner's social-anthropological narrative of Africa, a text he calls *The Pacification of the Primitive Tribes of the Lower Niger*, in which Okonkwo might form 'a reasonable paragraph' (148). This text is mentioned at the end of the novel, when the Umuofia villagers offer to pay the colonizers to bury Okonkwo because their tribal religious beliefs forbid them from touching a suicide. By contrast, the novel that precedes the District Commissioner's verdict is perceived from the perspective of a Nigerian, elevating an Ibo world-view above a Eurocentric one.

Things Fall Apart is the first novel in an 'Okonkwo Trilogy' that includes *No Longer at Ease* (1960) and *Arrow of God* (1964), and charts the breakdown of tribal loyalties. In the final novel in the series, set in the early 1920s when the colonial administration is firmly in place, *The Pacification of the Primitive Tribes of the Lower Niger* has already become a colonial classic. But it is in the second novel in the trilogy that Achebe most engages with *Heart of Darkness*. *No Longer at Ease*, itself a quotation from T. S. Eliot's 'The Journey of the Magi', is the story of Okonkwo's grandson, Obi, and the collapse of his idealism. Obi, who believes that the elimination of corruption in the country will follow once young, educated Nigerians take over posts in the civil service, is sponsored by his Umuofian villagers to travel to England to study law, so as to help them with village business in a changing world by assuming a post in the colonial administration. Obi, however, elects to study English. The tale, a prodigal's return, is embedded within a frame-narrative that describes Obi's trial for accepting bribes.

Besides passing an acerbic comment upon Nigerian politics in the year in which Nigeria achieved independence from Britain, the novel shows how his contact with Europe destroys Obi's identity and values, as his weakening command of his native tongue and sense of tribal ritual demonstrate when he returns. Dubbed Achebe's 'Heart of Whiteness', *No Longer at Ease* thus reverses the colonial trope of 'going native', with Obi presented as a parodic African Kurtz. Upon his return, Obi is feted by the villagers who identify themselves in terms that seem designed to recall the 'hollowness' of Kurtz: 'We are not empty men who become white when they see white, and black when they see black' (53).

Other African writers have also drawn upon Conrad's influence. For instance, Ngũgĩ's *A Grain of Wheat* (1967), set on the eve of Kenyan independence, is generally seen as a reworking of Conrad's *Under Western Eyes* (1911); while *Season of Migration to the North* (1969), by the Sudanese writer Tayeb Salih, reverses the colonial journey of Kurtz in its presentation of Mustafa's sexual exploitation of European women, which stands as a sort of post-colonial revenge. In each of these works, it is the European reader who is designated a peripheral vision, an excluded onlooker into formerly colonized cultures.

A twist on the post-colonial 'African' response is provided by the Trinidadian writer, V. S. Naipaul, whose portrait of an emergent Africa in *A Bend in the River* (1979) focuses upon Salim, an Indian trader who runs a small shop selling Western goods in Kisangani, the prototype for Kurtz's Inner Station, in the 1960s. The Kurtz-figure in the novel, known simply as the Big Man, is recognizable as President Mobuto, the first ruler of an independent Congo, whose increasing hold on power leads him to nationalize the businesses of foreigners, including Salim's shop, which passes to a semi-illiterate, alcoholic African. Trying to raise money in order to return to London to start a new life, Salim is betrayed to the police for secretly dealing in gold and ivory, and the book ends with his flight aboard the last steamer. Naipaul, who defended Conrad from Achebe's charge of racism, has himself drawn criticism from Achebe and others for his depiction of 'third world' stereotypes.

The powerful presence of the jungle and the river, together with the small trading outposts and official toll-posts, make the setting familiar to readers of *Heart of Darkness*. Like Marlow, Salim is forced to confront his dual identity as an insider and an outsider, and his journey into 'the heart of the continent' (Naipaul 1979: 52) is, similarly, one of disillusion that sustains a journey into the self and into African politics. Described as 'a truly remarkable man' (144), the Big Man's strong-arm tactics include dropping 'explosives at random in the bush' (87), reminding the reader of the French gunboat 'firing into a continent' in *Heart of Darkness* (62). Also, like Kurtz, he is a demagogue, addicted to words. His maxims adorn hoardings and walls, and are broadcast on the radio. Salim views these as 'the lies he started making us all live' (12). In this way, Naipaul uses *Heart of Darkness* as an enduring myth of political degeneracy. As this manifests itself in the breakdown of order, a fellow trader,

Mahesh, tells Salim: 'It isn't that there's no right and wrong here. There's no right' (102).

CONCLUSION

As these few examples demonstrate, the 'Conrad world' has been able to read and respond to his representation of it in various ways, including interrogative reaction, formal parody, and cultural absorption. To complete this survey of Conrad's influence. I shall return to Europe to offer a final intertextual example, William Golding's *Rites of Passage* (1980), that exploits the thematic and mythical dimensions of *Heart of Darkness*.

Set in the early nineteenth century, aboard an unnamed ship bound for Australia, Golding's novel charts the passage from European waters to the Equator. It is presented in the form of two interleaved narratives with contrasting world-views. The journal of Edmund Talbot, the supercilious godson of a peer, is couched in Augustan irony, while the letter of the immature Reverend James Colley, embedded within Talbot's journal, betrays a Romantic sensitivity. The increased victimization of Colley by the captain, which Talbot does nothing to prevent, leads to his humiliation by the crew at a crossing-the-line ceremony, as a result of which he dies of shame. Using a familiar Conradian trope, the tale thus charts the gradual breakdown of civilized values as the voyage into the unknown is fashioned as a voyage into the dark interior of the human landscape. In possession of a letter written by Colley to his sister, Talbot is placed in a moral dilemma similar to Marlow's at the end of *Heart of Darkness*. Should he inform her of the sordid events that led to her brother's death or protect her from knowledge of the evil at the centre of the human heart? In the event, his course of action might be construed as a more extreme, more morally reprehensible version of Marlow's: he resolves to write to her, telling her nothing but 'lies from beginning to end' (277).

Clearly designed to represent a 'slice of life', the ship is demarcated by a white line across the deck, separating the officers and privileged passengers from the crew and ordinary passengers. Significantly, crossing this line also leads to the dark place where

Colley will be debauched. Talbot also has to cross this line in order to get to the bilges, down in the 'foetid darkness' (83) of the ship. The doubling of Talbot and Colley presents a psychological pairing that bears comparison with the relationship between Marlow and Kurtz. As Marlow's journey to Kurtz progresses, so his realization of his own vulnerable humanity – what binds him to rather than separates him from Kurtz – deepens. Similarly, in *Rites of Passage*, Talbot is identified with his opposite. When Colley retreats to his cabin in shame, Talbot visits him there and realizes: 'Colley's hutch was the mirror image of mine' (131). Marlow and Talbot each gain personal insights from the death of their opposite numbers, who prove both objects of their narration and catalysts of their spiritual development.

The influence of *Heart of Darkness* upon subsequent writers has been profound and wide-ranging. Whether critical or reverential, their responses testify to the enduring power of Conrad's story. The reason for this is not hard to discern. According to C. B. Cox: 'This masterpiece has become one of those amazing modern fictions, such as Thomas Mann's *Death in Venice* or Kafka's *The Trial*, which throw light on the whole nature of twentieth-century art, its problems and achievements' (1974: vii).

QUESTIONS

1. Despite the continuing allure of Conrad's fiction to film-makers, few successful films have been made of his works. Suggest why this might be the case.
2. Explain why *Heart of Darkness* continues to inspire other writers and identify the ways in which two of them have responded to the novella in their writings.
3. Write a short outline of your own creative response to *Heart of Darkness* in any medium (such as film, fiction, drama, radio-script, or diary), together with a critique that identifies the problems you encountered and how you resolved these. You may wish to restrict yourself to a single scene.

CHAPTER 6

GUIDE TO FURTHER READING

CHAPTER 1: INTRODUCTION

Chesterton, G. K., *Heretics*. [1905] London: John Lane, 1928.

Edel, Leon (ed.), *Henry James Letters. Volume 4: 1895–1916*. Cambridge, Mass.: Belknap Press, 1984.

Hardy, Thomas, *Jude the Obscure* 'The New Wessex Edition'. London: Macmillan, 1990.

Hobsbawm, Eric, *The Age of Empire: 1875–1914*. London: Abacus, 2002.

Joyce, James, *Dubliners*. [1914] London: Jonathan Cape, 1971.

Lawrence, D. H., *Kangaroo*. [1923] London: William Heinemann, 1970.

Lycett, Andrew, *Rudyard Kipling*. London: Weidenfeld & Nicolson, 1999.

Matthew, H. C. G. and Kenneth O. Morgan, *The Oxford History of Britain: The Modern Age*. Oxford: Oxford University Press, 1992.

Najder, Żdzisław (ed.), *Conrad's Polish Background*. London: Oxford University Press, 1964.

—— (ed.), *Conrad under familial eyes*. Cambridge: Cambridge University Press, 1983.

Nietzsche, Friedrich, *Thus Spake Zarathustra*. [1883–91] Translated by A. Tille. London: J. M. Dent, 1933.

Pakenham, Thomas, *The Scramble for Africa: 1876–1912*. London: Weidenfeld and Nicolson, 1991.

Stape, J. H., and Owen Knowles (eds), *A Portrait in Letters:*

Correspondence To and About Conrad. Amsterdam: Rodopi, 1996.

Woolf, Virginia, *The Common Reader*. [1925] London: Hogarth Press, 1942.

—— *The Captain's Death Bed and Other Essays*. [1950] London: Hogarth Press, 1981.

—— *Congenial Spirits: Selected Letters*. London: Hogarth Press, 1993.

CHAPTER 2: LANGUAGE, STYLE AND FORM

Beckett, Samuel, *Proust*. London: Calder & Boyars, 1965.

Conrad, John, *Joseph Conrad: Times Remembered.* Cambridge: Cambridge University Press, 1981.

James, Henry, *Literary Criticism: Volume One*. New York: Library of America, 1984.

Leavis, F. R., *The Great Tradition: George Eliot, Henry James, Joseph Conrad.* London: Chatto & Windus, 1948.

Najder, Zdzisław, *Joseph Conrad: A Chronicle*. Cambridge: Cambridge University Press, 1983.

Ray, Martin (ed.), *Joseph Conrad: Interviews and Recollections*. London: Macmillan, 1990.

Renoir, Jean, *Renoir, My Father*. Translated by Randolph and Dorothy Weaver. London: Collins, 1962.

Watt, Ian, *Conrad in the Nineteenth Century*. London: Chatto & Windus, 1980.

Woolf, Virginia, *The Common Reader*. [1925] London: Hogarth Press, 1942.

CHAPTER 3: READING *HEART OF DARKNESS*

Boswell, James, *The Life of Samuel Johnson, LL.D.* Vol. 1. [1791] Edited by Percy Fitzgerald. London: George Allen & Unwin, 1924.

Conrad, Joseph, *Congo Diary*. Edited by Zdzisław Najder. New York: Doubleday, 1978.

Dante, *The Divine Comedy*. Translated by C. H. Sisson. Manchester: Carcanet, 1980.

Eliot, T. S., *The Complete Poems and Plays of T. S. Eliot*. London: Faber and Faber, 1969.

Guerard, Albert J., *Conrad the Novelist*. Cambridge, Mass.: Harvard University Press, 1958.

Ibsen, Hendrik, *The Wild Duck* [1884] in *Plays: One*. Translated by Michael Meyer. London: Methuen, 1980.

Kingsley, Mary, *Travels in West Africa*. London: Macmillan, 1897.

Sherry, Norman, *Conrad's Western World*. Cambridge: Cambridge University Press, 1971.

Smith, Walter E., *Joseph Conrad: A Bibliographical Catalogue of his Major First Editions with Facsimiles of Several Title Pages*. Long Beach, California: Privately printed, n.d.

Watts, Cedric, *The Deceptive Text: An Introduction to Covert Plots*. Brighton: Harvester, 1984.

CHAPTER 4: CRITICAL RECEPTION AND PUBLISHING HISTORY

Achebe, Chinua, *Hopes and Impediments: Selected Essays*. London: Anchor Books, 1989.

Alden, W. L., *The New York Times Book Review*. 11 March 1899: 160; 6 May 1899: 304; 17 June 1899: 388; 13 December 1902: 10.

Baines, Jocelyn, *Joseph Conrad*. London: Weidenfeld, 1960.

Firchow, Peter Edgerly, *Envisioning Africa: Racism and Imperialism in Conrad's 'Heart of Darkness'*. Lexington: University of Kentucky Press, 1999.

Forster, E. M., *Abinger Harvest*. Harmondsworth: Penguin, 1974.

Galsworthy, John, *Castles in Spain and Other Screeds*. London: Heinemann, 1927.

Gordan, John Dozier, *Joseph Conrad: The Making of a Novelist*. Cambridge, Mass.: Harvard University Press, 1940.

Guerard, Albert J., *Conrad the Novelist*. Cambridge, Mass.: Harvard University Press, 1958.

Gurko, Leo, *Joseph Conrad: Giant in Exile*. London: Macmillan, 1960.

Hay, Eloise Knapp, *The Political Novels of Joseph Conrad: A Critical Study*. Chicago: University of Chicago Press, 1963.

Jameson, Frederick, *The Political Unconscious: Narrative as a Socially Symbolic Act*. London: Methuen, 1981.

Johnson, Bruce, *Conrad's Models of Mind*. Minneapolis: University of Minnesota Press, 1971.

Karl, Frederick R., *Joseph Conrad: The Three Lives*. London: Faber and Faber, 1979.

Kirschner, Paul, *Conrad: The Psychologist as Artist*. Edinburgh: Oliver & Boyd, 1968.

Leavis, F. R., *The Great Tradition: George Eliot, Henry James, Joseph Conrad*. London: Chatto & Windus, 1948.

Moser, Thomas C., *Joseph Conrad: Achievement and Decline*. Cambridge, Mass.: Harvard University Press, 1957.

Nadelhaft, Ruth, *Joseph Conrad*. Hemel Hempstead: Harvester Wheatsheaf, 1991.

Nazareth, Peter, 'Out of Darkness: Conrad and Other Third World Writers'. *Conradiana* 14 (1983): 173–87.

Palmer, John A., *Joseph Conrad's Fiction: A Study in Literary Growth*. New York: Cornell University Press, 1968.

Saveson, John E., *Joseph Conrad: The Making of a Moralist*. Amsterdam: Rodopi, 1972.

Smith, Johanna M., 'Too Beautiful Altogether: Patriarchal Ideology in *Heart of Darkness*' in Ross C. Murfin (ed.), *Joseph Conrad 'Heart of Darkness': A Case Study in Contemporary Criticism*. 179–95. New York: St. Martin's Press, 1989.

Smith, Steve, 'Marxism and Ideology: Joseph Conrad, *Heart of Darkness*' in Douglas Tallack (ed.), *Literary Theory at Work*. London: Batsford, 1987.

Straus, Nina Pelikan, 'The Exclusion of the Intended from Secret Sharing in Conrad's *Heart of Darkness*'. *Novel* 20 (1987): 123–37.

Thorburn, David, *Conrad's Romanticism*. New Haven, CT: Yale University Press, 1974.

Watt, Ian, *Conrad in the Nineteenth Century*. London: Chatto & Windus, 1979.

Yelton, Donald C., *Mimesis and Metaphor: An Inquiry into the Genesis and Scope of Conrad's Symbolic Imagery*. The Hague: Mouton, 1967.

CHAPTER 5: ADAPTATION, INTERPRETATION AND INFLUENCE

Achebe, Chinua, *Things Fall Apart*. [1958] London: Heinemann: 1986.

—— *No Longer at Ease*. London: Heinemann, 1960.

—— *Arrow of God*. London: Heinemann, 1964.

—— *Hopes and Impediments: Selected Essays*. London: Anchor Books, 1989.

Ballantyne, J. M., *The Coral Island*. London: 1857.

Beerbohm, Max, *A Christmas Garland*. [1912] New Haven: Yale University Press, 1993.

Bloom, Harold, *The Anxiety of Influence: A Theory of Poetry*. Oxford: Oxford University Press, 1973.

Boehmer, Elleke (ed.), *Empire Writing: An Anthology of Colonial Literature 1870–1918*. Oxford: Oxford University Press, 1998.

Cox, C. B., 'Introduction' in *Joseph Conrad, Youth: A Narrative / Heart of Darkness / The End of the Tether*. London: Dent, 1974.

Downes, Olin, 'Music'. *The New York Times*, 25 April 1929: 32.

Eliot, T. S., *The Complete Poems and Plays of T. S. Eliot*. London: Faber and Faber, 1969.

—— *Selected Essays*. London: Faber and Faber, 1980.

Gary, Romain, *La Nuit sera calme*. Paris: Gallimard, 1974.

Gide, André, *Voyage au Congo*. Paris: Gallimard, 1927.

Golding, William, *Lord of the Flies* (1954).

—— *Rites of Passage*. London: Faber & Faber, 1980.

Greene, Graham, *A Burnt-out Case*. [1961] London: Bodley Head, 1974.

—— *In Search of a Character*. Harmondsworth: Penguin, 1968.

Joyce, James, *A Portrait of the Artist as a Young Man*. [1916] London: Jonathan Cape, 1968.

Lindqvist, Sven, '*Exterminate All the Brutes*'. London: Granta, 1997.

Ludwig, Richard M. (ed.), *Letters of Ford Madox Ford*. Princeton: Princeton University Press, 1965.

Najder, Zdzisław (ed.), *Conrad under familial eyes*. Cambridge: Cambridge University Press, 1983.

Naipaul, V. S., *A Bend in the River*. London: Andre Deutsch, 1979.

Ngũgĩ, *A Grain of Wheat*. London: Heinemann, 1967.

Orwell, George, *The Collected Essays, Journalism and Letters of George Orwell. Volume 4: In Front of Your Nose 1945–1950*. [1968] Harmondsworth: Penguin, 1978.

Randall, Dale B. J. (ed.), *Joseph Conrad and Warrington Dawson: The Record of a Friendship*. Durham, NC: Duke University Press, 1968.

Said, Edward, *Orientalism: Western Conceptions of the Orient*. [1978] London: Penguin, 1991.

Salih, Tayeb, *Season of Migration to the North*. [1969] London: Heinemann, 1991.

Stape, J. H. (ed.), *The Cambridge Companion to Joseph Conrad*. Cambridge: Cambridge University Press, 1996.

Steiner, George, *Real Presences*. London: Faber and Faber, 1989.

White, William (ed.), *By-Line: Ernest Hemingway: Selected Articles and Dispatches of Four Decades*. New York: Bantam paperback, 1968, 114–15.

Williams, Anne, *Art of Darkness: A Poetics of Gothic*. Chicago: University of Chicago Press, 1995.

Woolf, Virginia, *The Captain's Death Bed and Other Essays*. [1950] London: Hogarth Press, 1981.

INDEX